Freud and the Invention of Jewishness

THE SEA HORSE IMPRINT

Paola Mieli, *Publisher and Director*
Mark Stafford, *Editorial Director*
David Jacobson, *Manuscript Editor*
Richard G. Klein, *Research and Bibliography*

This book is published under the aegis and with the financial assistance of Après-Coup Psychoanalytic Association, New York.

Cover image:
Plancius, Geography of the Exodus (ca. 1590)

Betty Bernardo Fuks

Freud and the Invention of Jewishness

Translated by Paulo Henriques Britto

Agincourt Press
New York, 2008

Originally published in Portuguese as *Freud e a judeidade, a vocação do exilio*
ISBN 978-1-946328-58-8 (paper) Copyright © by Betty Fuks 2008

Design and typesetting
Danilo Montanari

Agincourt Press
P.O. Box 1039
Cooper Station
New York, NY 10003
www.agincourtpress.org

*To my grandchildren,
Júlia, Gabriel, Milla, Tamara, and Bernardo*

EDITORIAL NOTE

Freud's title *Der Mann Moses und die monotheistische Religion* translates, literally, as "Moses the Man and the Monotheistic Religion." The English rendition as "Moses and Monotheism" is an accepted but misleading interpretation. It is our task to stress the significance of Freud's own chosen words, especially when there are no particular obstacles to translating them. It is the task of the analyst to read according to the letter. Had Freud wished to call his study *Moses und der Monotheismus*, he could have done so. This would have been tantamount to underlining the figure of Moses as a mythical, religious, or subjectively interpreted character. To respect and restore the author's intention of emphasizing his subject's particular, concrete, and real connotations, as well as the historical advent of monotheistic religion, we will refer in this book to Freud's work by its original title, *Der Mann Moses und die monotheistische Religion*.

Table of Contents

9   Foreword by Paola Mieli

17 Introduction

23 Chapter 1. Strategies of Resistance

47 Chapter 2. Reading Freud, Psychoanalysis, and Judaism

65 Chapter 3. Exile and Foreignness

91 Chapter 4. YHWH, the Stranger of Strangers

103 Chapter 5. Interpretation: Wandering and the Nomadism of the Letter

119 Conclusion

123 Bibliography

Foreword
Paola Mieli

To return to Freud, to the clinical and intellectual path he opened in discovering psychoanalysis, to re-examine his thought, his hesitations, his insights, is a necessary practice for any psychoanalyst, since formation in the discipline is inseparable from the study of its foundations. Evidence of such a return to Freud and its impact on the reflection of a particular analyst is a valuable element for understanding an aspect of the vicissitudes of transmission, a transmission that implies, among other things, a transferential relation to the founding texts, a philological reading of those texts as well as a unique appropriation of them. It is no accident that, bearing this in mind we have chosen this book by Betty B. Fuks to launch a series of texts not so much "of" or "on" psychoanalysis, but of interest for analytic work, for analysts and for anyone who reflects on the impact of psychoanalysis on the thought of our time.

Such a choice has to do with the very question this book addresses, a question that has been with psychoanalysis since its inception, namely, that of the influence of Jewish culture on its discovery and conceptualization; it has to do with its methodology, which in proposing to "read Freud with Freud," seeks to distance itself both from psychobiography and from readings that tend to "Judaize psychoanalysis or psychoanalyze Judaism"; and it most certainly has to do with the interest of its conclusions, which, in taking up the thread of the well-known initiatives of several authors – Lévinas, Yerushalmi, Blanchot, Jabès, de Certeau, Derrida – advances positions that subvert any number of commonplaces on the relation between psychoanalysis and Judaism, and lead to fruitful, original reflection. An original and startlingly obvious reflection, as is often the case with conclusions which, deriving from subjective experience, immediately come to seem self-evident, as if they had always been known.

Such is the case with the central theses Fuks develops. *Jewishness*, as distinguished from Judaism, is not a state, a given essence, but rather an evolving practice, a "construction" that establishes a precise ethical position and a foundation for psychoanalysis, defining both its practice and its forms of transmission. Freud's atheism, with its origins in and its distance from a given culture, calls into play this *Jewishness*, and thereby instigates a radically new way of conceptualizing subjectivity, an unprecedented listening to subjective suffering. If an affiliation, or transferential relation, between Jewish culture and psychoanalysis is to be posited, such a relation must focus on Judaism's intrinsic atheism: that is, an ethical position, which in fleeing the idolatry of an ultimate truth, of a given representation or a once-and-for-all acquired meaning, consistently interrogates the text to produce new readings, fostering the very practice of reading. This is a position bolstered by Freud's notion of science as a system of thought that, unlike religion, includes hypothesis, error, the unknown, and is based on assumptions that allow for their own refutability. It is a position, therefore, opposed to any form of ultimate certainty and fundamentalism, if we hold to the notion that where reading ends, idolatry begins.

Fuks points out how psychoanalysis recognizes in an inherent feature of Jewish experience, namely Diaspora, or forced exile, an aspect of human subjectivity in general, and extracts from it a structural element of its practice: the formations of the unconscious attest to the division of the subject, to the presence of an unconscious knowledge that incessantly produces effects in daily life. The course of a cure leads into foreign terrain, into unknown places that intimately belong to the subject. Psychoanalysis involves exile from the mystifying identifications that keep the symptom in place, moving in the direction of a progressive deconstruction of "narcissistic idolatry and the mandates of the superego." It entails, essentially, openness toward what is other. In renewing the long Western tradition that viewed Moses as an Egyptian, Freud placed at the core of his reading of Jewish history a foundation based on difference – a foundation based on the relation to what is (even ethnically) other, thereby establishing an intrinsic relationship between Judaism and Jewishness. And this is a suggestion that, symptomatically, has become a source of permanent scandal to many.

Last but not least, Fuks posits that the Freudian notion of memory finds its roots in a tradition that considers the practice of recollection an ethical commitment, a commitment that, in linking the future with the past, transforms the present, ensuring transmission between generations.

There is no need to belabor here the motivations and articulations in Fuks's thought, which she herself has clearly outlined in her introduction. Yet it does warrant attention that this book is the first draft of a project whose rationale and form are to be found in the process of its elaboration. If indeed certain ideas and quotations aren't fully developed, this has the advantage of showing the matrix of reflection from which Fuks has since drawn substance for a series of articles that have had international resonance. Readers have access, then, to a work in progress, with all its insights and limitations, a work essential for understanding an author's progress, her bibliographical references, and the unfolding of her thought.

Choosing to open this publication series with a work in progress also means taking a stance in a publishing world that, in the realm of the scholarly essay, grants space only to edited and re-edited texts. If the advantage of good editorial guidance is that it pushes an author further along the path of his or her thought, the disadvantage of the publishing world's smug stereotyping is the recourse to writing norms that, for the sake of clarity and conformity, flatten and distort both an author's style and line of investigation, often stifling his or her voice – a voice sometimes heard most clearly in its hesitations, contradictions and repetitions, and unfinished utterances. Often it is only through its success abroad that editors decide to publish an essay of unconventional form. Undoubtedly, an essay such as *Der Mann Moses und die monotheistische Religion* – to stay within our subject-matter and cite a writer of talent whose work remains the source of all sorts of studies and reflections – would never have been accepted first by an American academic press.

Form, however, is part of content, and singularity of style is what allows for both transmission and the possible emergence of original thinking. Analytical practice, which is a practice of listening and reading – as Fuks emphasizes in her book – demonstrates how its success and its transmission results in a style: the unique, singular style of a particular person.

To understand the analytic path and its characteristic ethics, one must, however, grasp its specificity. For the American public familiar with all sorts of therapeutic promises and a psychoanalytic tradition far removed from Freudian foundations, it is worth remembering that psychoanalysis is not "a form of individual psychotherapy" devoted to "improving adaptation" and "alleviating the symptoms of mental disorder."[1] To consider a symptom the sign of a mental "disorder" means hypostatizing a given neurophysiological order, consistent with a medically inspired mechanistic determinism that reveals the persistence of a nineteenth-century conception of psychic functioning, a conception that predates Freud's

---

[1] This is the notion expressed in the 2001 "Standards of Psychoanalytic Education" of The Psychoanalytic Consortium (comprising: the American Psychoanalytic Association, the American Academy of Psychoanalysis, the National Membership Committee on Psychoanalysis in Clinical Social Work, and Division 39 of the American Psychological Association).

discovery of the formations of the unconscious and bypasses them altogether. Freud showed – and this is the very foundation of psychoanalysis – that the relation between primary and secondary processes is articulated and decipherable according to the specificity inherent in psychic causality. He showed that the symptom, far from being the sign of a mental disorder, is the result of a precise order, the expression of specific reactive formations that convey a subjective truth. By introducing the difference between instinct and drive, need and desire, he showed that the body cannot be reduced to its organic materiality; that physiological reality is accompanied by the shaping of the subjective body as an effect of the drive circuit. He showed that genetic, physiological, and environmental factors are necessary but not sufficient conditions for understanding the specificity of the human psyche, and that one must add to them the understanding of the causality proper to the psyche's structure.

Unlike the pharmacological/therapeutic promise of alleviating or suppressing symptoms, the analytic cure posits the transformation of the drive economy those symptoms express. As opposed to an ideology of mass medicalization that exempts patients from subjective responsibility – a normative response – analytic practice posits the assumption of a precise position: that in which subjects assume the very causes of which they are an effect. They make themselves responsible for their own destiny. A clear distinction must be drawn here between morals and ethics: the former representing rules of conduct in service to an ideology, a faith, or a group's interests; the latter being the expression of what regulates a specific way of doing something, preserving its particularity and regulating the relation of that doing with the community in which it is inscribed. A morality is the fruit of an externally imposed code; an ethics, the product of the internal rigor of a given practice.

It is worth rereading *The Question of Lay Analysis*, which alludes, among other things, to the American deviation, to see that Freud understands the position of the analyst above all as an ethical one, the result of a subjective transformation that evolves in relation to what is presented as Other. It is surely not the result of a series of procedures devoted to a practical expertise, as implied in the Anglo-Saxon application of the term "training" to an analyst's preparation, which likens it to that of other professions. As any analyst who is an analyst knows, becoming an analyst implies a route and a temporality that vary from individual to individual, unlike other forms of professional apprenticeship. It would be useful, then, to reclaim the etymological use of the word "formation" (from the Greek *morphe* and the Latin *forma*), which, as Webster's indicates, designates "the act of creating or causing to exist": at once an unfolding process and its outcome.

The word has its specific weight, as all words do. One may well wonder to what extent the casual use of the term "training" indicates a concession that, in stressing professional apprenticeship rather than a process of subjective transformation, marks a difference of points of view – and a difference in listening to subjective suffering.

In *The Question of Lay Analysis* Freud's imaginary dialogue with his "impartial" interlocutor leads, as in a psychoanalytic situation, to a question: a question of knowledge. It is in this framework – the framework of transference – that Freud sets the commonplaces about an analyst's formation. The impartial interlocutor speaks like someone who, while knowing nothing about psychoanalysis, nonetheless knows how someone should become an analyst. He occupies the subjective position of prejudice human beings commonly hold when confronted with the unknown. Confronted with difference in the real.

Freud responds by summing up the key points of analytic theory; its goal is to signify the division of the subject, and thus signify how the transmission of psychoanalysis cannot be reduced to the pure learning of an academic or technical knowledge, since the psychic structure marks out an irreducible difference between knowledge and truth. It is this very difference that founds analytic practice, the difference by virtue of which Freud can enunciate the fundamental rule of speech in analysis: that of saying whatever comes to mind, "Sagen Sie also alles, was Ihnen durch den Sinn geht." And he adds: "In confession the sinner tells all he knows; in analysis the neurotic has to say much more."

In introducing existent but unknown knowledge, the fundamental rule gives a status and a presence in the analytical framework to the "other scene," *der andere Schauplatz*, as Freud terms the unconscious. Automatically, then, transference cannot be reduced to a dual relation, since it is defined by the presence of what is Other, the presence summoned by the act of speech, according to the trinary nature of human language.[2] Counterpart to the fundamental rule is a listening governed by what Freud defines as "gleichschwebende Aufmerksamkeit," an *evenly* floating attention (and stress should fall on the evenness, the equality in level of listening). The

---

[2] As opposed to its logical or technological reduction into a binary code – the "either/or" solution – the trinary nature of human language is characterized by bringing absence into presence (as indicated in the usage of the third-person pronoun and the possibility of condensing a plurality of meanings into a metaphor).

product of the subjective experience of separation between knowing and truth, such listening is guided by the uniqueness of the analysand's speech – not the dictates of the theory. A fine ear for unconscious processes, as Freud calls it, is geared toward the logical rigor of the concatenation of signifiers produced in the transference, toward what produces effects of sense, or non-sense, beyond the intentions of discourse. It is geared toward the act of speech, which in implying a gap between the subject of enunciation and the subject of the statement, between saying and the said, allows for the emergence of the subject of desire, which underlies symptoms, inhibitions, anxieties, and the formations of the unconscious in general. It is such an emergence that gives the cure a precise direction – an aim and a possible end.

Analysts thus find themselves occupying a peculiar position, like that of a ballerina poised on a single toe, to borrow a metaphor from *Der Mann Moses und die monotheistische Religion*; a position at once rigorous and evolving, incessantly taking shape in relation to the uniqueness of their act. An act performed, by definition, in difference; it is no accident that Freud urges analysts to start each new analysis as though it were the first. If analytical formation requires a vast field of disciplines – from science to the history of religion, from medicine to anthropology, to philosophy, to literature and art (far vaster, no doubt, than that of the disciplines commonly listed in "training institutes") – if it implies a strict, ceaseless relation to knowing, it also implies learning to have a relation to knowledge that does not hypostatize it: that knows how to discard that knowledge, how to shed it in the course of its act and allow for a listening that is always fresh. It is this atheistic, humble position toward knowledge, toward a knowledge that continually opens itself to a new knowing, which Fuks calls an evolving *Jewishness*.

"Judaism requires that its interpreter assume the position of the atheist, one who will not block the advent of the word, making a golden calf out of the text." If a methodological affinity exists between the ethics of Talmudic interpretation and analytical practice, it must be stressed that the reading or interpretation at work in the "talking cure" has an aim and an end all its own: the text is offered by the analysand's speech and silences, what *does not* allow just any type of reading or interpretation, but rather a *specific* reading dictated by the concatenation of signifiers and its inherent letters. However plural this may be – given the overdetermined character of the formations of the unconscious – it is not "infinite," because it operates within a *specific* transferential relation and has a direction of its own, toward the emptying of registers of meaning proper to the subject's symptoms and compulsory repetitions, toward the deconstruction of the libidinal economy that structures them. It goes in the direction of the emergence of a new significance, in anticipation of new significations.

Fuks rightly wonders whether a certain institutionalization of psychoanalysis, by denaturing it, doesn't also spell its doom, whether it doesn't, indeed, prevent its transmission. This is a question all the more crucial in the current social situation, in which conflicts of interest between psychoanalytical groups lead to state intervention, called in to regulate the profession. But if psychoanalysts are not able to maintain and regulate their own practice, if they yield to factional fights and power struggles rather than forming a common front in the face of social transformations and demands, in the face of spreading (pseudo-)scientific discourse that forecloses the subject of the unconscious and promotes the business of mass medicalization, this proves that they have not met their responsibilities and that analytic transmission has not taken place. Returning to question the nature of psychoanalysis and the ways of its transmission, to re-establish its premises, is therefore a necessary exercise.

In an era that tends toward immediate answers and instant gratifications, be they therapeutic, pharmacological, scientific, religious, or ideological, in an era that silences the encounter with the limits of the knowable through production of idols of every type, psychoanalysis is confirmed in its anti-idolatrous marginal position – a position of exile that, as Fuks stresses, is both its nature and its strength. This is the position from which it ceaselessly renews its own transmission.

Introduction

> *Exile was perhaps the first issue, for exile was the first word – before-the-exile is before-the-word.*
>
> EDMOND JABÈS, *Le Livre des Ressemblances*

My original project – to attempt to answer the difficult and recurrent question of the traces of Jewish culture in psychoanalysis – began to take shape when I decided to enroll in the School of Communications at the Universidade Federal do Rio de Janeiro for my Ph.D. I chose this institution because its transdisciplinary program emphasizes a continuous, fluid, and fruitful exchange between several of the most significant manifestations of classical and contemporary thought. It seemed to me that this kind of training would enrich the inevitably tortuous paths one must follow when desire forces one to seek words to speak about something that remains obscure and elusive.

I began by taking an oblique and indirect approach. At first, perhaps excited by the mirror-image fascination brought about by my immersion in the various authors who had previously discussed this issue, I tried to articulate Judaism and psychoanalysis through the method of comparison between Jewish culture and Freud's discovery. But gradually I became enmeshed in and overwhelmed by the immense exegesis I had been led into by my own prejudices and by everything that had been said about the topic. To avoid repetition, I was forced to change my course dramatically and risk facing the unknown, acknowledging the vastness of this protean object that is Judaism. So I decided to find out in what ways Freud was close to it and what effect it might have had on the clinical practice he invented.

The effort to remain faithful to the radicalness of psychoanalysis, to listen to the subject and to culture, finally led me to what I now believe to be the only possible way to proceed on the basis of my initial hypothesis: an archaeology[1] of the culture of Judaism and psychoanalysis could

---

[1] As used in this work, "archaeology" refers to a notion inspired by the concept intro-

be accomplished only if conducted according to Goethe's maxim quoted by Freud in *Totem and Taboo*: "What thou hast inherited from thy fathers, acquire it to make it thine."² So it was that I began to formulate a number of contingent answers to what only later (*nachträglich*) I realized was the core of my hypothesis. Freud's *becoming-Jew* – something that is radically differentiated from his Jewish condition, for what is at stake here is not so much the accidental circumstance of his birth as the future of what he strove to shape – found in psychoanalysis its ultimate expression as the practice of the non-identical, of de-identification and of the desire for difference. To think about how Freud exerted his "Jewishness" protects psychoanalysis from the mystification of its alleged Jewish origin and demonstrates the contingency that led a godless Jew, as Freud described himself, to create psychoanalysis and preserve its future.

The terms "Judaism," "Jewry," and "Jewishness" are used in this book in accordance with the definitions proposed by Albert Memmi in the first chapter of *L'Homme dominé*: "Judaism" means "the set of cultural and religious traditions"; "Jewry" (the French *judaïcité*) refers specifically to the totality of the Jewish people as a demographic reality, scattered in various communities around the world; "Jewishness" (*judéité*) alludes exclusively to the fact of feeling Jewish, "the way in which a Jew is Jewish, subjectively and objectively." Memmi coins the term *judéité* to speak about the way in which each Jew *experiences* his or her own Jewish condition. Jewishness should be understood as something that must always be defined and constructed and never finished, even for those for whom Judaism as a religion is not relevant. In this context one is reminded of Jacques Derrida's definition of Jewishness, in his foreword to *Mal d'archive* (*Archive Fever*), as an expression that inaugurates an act, a way of becoming another.

---

duced by Michel Foucault: simultaneous continuity and discontinuity between epistemes, i.e., unconscious structures in the sphere of knowledge that determine the ways in which objects are perceived, grouped together and defined. Each historical region of the episteme is the locus for a restructuring directed (but not organized) by the structures elaborated in the earlier era, which means that certain primitive scenes inhabit and determine a development that will destroy homogeneity. Each epistemological time carries within it an alterity, a difference. See Foucault, *Les Mots et les choses* (*The Order of Things: An Archaeology of Human Sciences*).

² Goethe, *Faust*, Part I, Scene 1, quoted in Sigmund Freud, *Standard Edition of the Complete Psychological Works*, trans. and ed. by James Strachey. (hereafter as *SE*), vol. 13, p. 158. [*Totem and Taboo*]

I was compelled to begin this study, and the reflections that resulted in the writing of this book, by two observations made by Freud that significantly referred to the circumstance of being a Jew. The first was his comment about the influence of his early absorption of Biblical history on his intellectual formation, and the second was his acknowledgment of the fact as a member of the Jewish minority he learned to resist in isolation, something that turned out to be extremely positive preparation for his struggle against internal and external resistances to psychoanalysis. In this way, I gradually came to see that there was a link between these statements, a link that provided a guideline for my work, which repeatedly rereads and reinterprets one with the help of the other in the pages that follow.

It is generally recognized that psychoanalysis made a decisive contribution, however contested, to the development of a critique of many prejudices. It is also acknowledged that the social, cultural, and personal exclusion experienced by Freud as a Diaspora Jew, who lived and worked under the special circumstances of turn-of-the-century Vienna, was of fundamental importance to the constitution of psychoanalytic practice and theory. But the cultural experience inscribed in the life and career of the discoverer of the psychoanalytic method was more than simply a historical factor to which he submitted passively. Indeed, the intimate impact of this Jewish heritage on Freud and his transformative response to it greatly helped him to progressively resolve the constitution of his own Jewishness and to establish strategies for fighting and tolerating the resistances to psychoanalysis.

In the discourse of turn-of-the-century European culture, when Freud wrote *The Interpretation of Dreams*, a work he considered to be the cornerstone of psychoanalysis, the category of the Jew was one of the specters of the Other that haunted the majorities in European countries, such that each Jew came to see him or herself as both a victim and a hero of the process of political modernization that had begun in the Enlightenment – an aspect of which had been the emancipation of the Jews. The course I embarked on in order to collect the material for what turned out to be the first chapter of this book, was to research Freud's reception of his Jewish upbringing, to investigate which factors of the social and cultural movement might have influenced his formation, and to discover some of the ways in which Freud came to particularize and subjectivize a heritage he never attempted to deny.

A bibliographical survey was necessary to find a methodology that would help me to remain faithful to the letter of Freud's text and to my own psychoanalytic practice. The tendency to subject Freud to psychobiography, to Judaize psychoanalysis and psychoanalyze Judaism – so common in psychoanalytic literature, in histories of psychoanalysis, and in biographies of Freud – were perhaps the greatest temptations I had to face until I was able to read Freud *with* Freud: that is, to read only his words and respect his silences. Some authors guided me in this task, a task that forced me to simultaneously rethink my own Jewishness and my condition as psychoanalyst, as one who must reinvent oneself at each session, at each sudden interruption of a treatment, at each termination of a treatment. For psychoanalysis, being a science of the particular, forces analysts to commit themselves to the art and the rigor of listening, as well as to creativity and the respect for singularity.

Among the texts I relied on, pride of place goes to the works of Emmanuel Lévinas, which are marked by an extraordinary balance between the discourse of Western philosophy and the specificity of the Jewish ethics of opening to the Other. Lévinas guided me in my reading of texts about Judaism, and also provided me a general orientation for the parallels and distinctions that I set up between psychoanalysis and Judaism. The works of the historian Yosef Hayim Yerushalmi had a decisive influence on the path I set out on in this book. In addition to inspiring me with his contributions concerning the singularity of Jewish historiography, Yerushalmi was also of great importance because of his translation and analysis of the Hebrew dedication Jakob Freud wrote for his son in the family Bible.

This, in turn, led me to study the relationship between Jews and writing, which brought me to the work of Jacques Derrida. Derrida's practice of deconstructing texts through critical reading greatly helped me to analyze the issues raised in the book, particularly with regard to the way in which the memory of the Jewish people is produced and to the function of memory in the psychoanalytic process.

In the return to Freud proposed by Jacques Lacan – which implied a critical overview of the deflections from Freud's ideas that post-Freudian theories had undergone and a radical revision of their understanding of the place of the analyst – I was able to find invaluable insights for the construction of the object of the present work. Lacan's observations concerning the presence of traces of Hebrew reading and writing in psychoanalysis were some of the byways that I explored in order to listen to the echoes of the particular modes of Jewish interpretation of sacred texts that resonate in the logic of psychoanalytic interpretation.

I offer my reading of Freud's *Der Mann Moses und die monotheistische Reli-*

gion (1939) taking into account the fact that the Old Testament is the point of departure for the ethics, aesthetics, religion, and politics of the Jewish people. In Chapter 3 I analyze some Biblical texts in which the Jewish people's choice of foreignness is associated with the search for difference and with the unshakable faith in the unknowable. The fact that nomadism and wandering precede sedentarization in Jewish history and the valorization of the figure of the foreigner in the Book of Books, guided my reading of *Der Mann Moses und die monotheistische Religion*. To claim that the Jewish people's greatest prophet was in fact a foreigner, an Egyptian, and not a Hebrew – the central claim in Freud's book – is perfectly in keeping with the Biblical ethos: Abraham, the patriarch of the Jewish people, the Moabite Ruth, the matriarch of Jewish royalty, and Jacob, who struggles with the Unknown, the angel of a Foreign God, all express the requirement of foreignness (*étrangeté*) that can be found in the writings of the earliest Hebrew writers.

The Biblical text not only assigns capital importance to what is foreign but also to the astounding idea of a God made of nothing, pure absence: nameless, faceless, with no image or essence. Mosaic doctrine is the expression of a dramatic abyss separating man from the deity, in which the word becomes the endless thread that weaves into a narrative the persistent void that exists between God and man, and between man and man. In Chapter 4 I attempt to grasp the echoes of this conception in Freud's discovery. Finally, Chapter 5 explores the similarities between Jewish reading of texts and psychoanalytic reading. In Jewish reading, it is the absent sign that engenders discourse and promotes interpretation. The Hebrew text, in its original form, is not given in its entirety, and the word can be read only taking into account its context. Similarly, psychoanalytic listening to the formations of the unconscious implies reading both presence and absence within the particular context in which the signifiers and the letters appear. Both practices of reading promote uniqueness and difference. They establish a non-dogmatic relation to knowledge.

Chapter 1
Strategies of Resistance

> *Two themes run through these pages: the story of my life and the history of psychoanalysis. They are intimately interwoven.*
>
> SIGMUND FREUD[1]

In order to understand how Freud invented his own Jewishness, and appreciate how this contributed to the discoveries of psychoanalysis, we must first delimit the historical and cultural milieu in which he lived. This requires reflecting on events that left a decisive mark on the Jewish communities in Europe and on Freud's Jewishness.

The best point of departure is Freud's own *An Autobiographical Study* (1925). "I was born on May 6th, 1856, at Freiberg in Moravia, a small town in what is now Czechoslovakia. My parents were Jewish, and I have remained a Jew myself. I have reason to believe that my father's family were settled for a long time on the Rhine." A few lines later Freud sketches a brief inventory of some of the moves endured by his family, which, "as a result of persecution of the Jews during the fourteenth or fifteenth century... fled eastwards, [and] in the course of the nineteenth century... migrated back from Lithuania through Galicia into German Austria."[2]

What is most striking about this text is that Freud emphasizes the exodus and exile his family experienced before settling down to a sedentary life. These experiences, which have been the typical lot of Jewish people from time immemorial, would also characterize the history of psychoanalysis from its origins in Vienna to Freud's final exile in London.

Promises and Victories: A Prophecy in the Park

Freud's first experience of exodus was a consequence of the dra-

---

[1] *SE*, vol. 20, p. 71. [*An Autobiographical Study*]
[2] Ibid., p. 10.

matic economic circumstances that befell his father's business. Around the middle of the nineteenth century Jakob Freud left the town of Freiberg with his family, briefly stayed in Leipzig, and then resettled in Vienna, a cradle of modernity.[3] The Freuds first went to live in the traditional Jewish district of Leopoldstadt, where nearly all Jewish migrants from the Austro-Hungarian Empire ended up, turning it into virtually a new ghetto.[4] In Vienna, Freud's parents, who came from the ghettos of West Galicia, became part of the *Ostjuden* population – East European Jews, who were by and large Orthodox and spoke Yiddish.[5]

Yiddish originated around the tenth century in Lotharingia (Lorraine), and its growth was deeply marked by its compound nature: it incorporated elements of a number of different languages, such as Hebrew, Laaz – a Hebraized Romance language spoken in this region – and Middle High German, as well as a number of Slavic tongues. The extraordinarily hybrid character of Yiddish may be seen in the following example given by Max Weinrich: "Nokkn bentshn hot der zeyde gekoyfte a seyfer" is a sentence meaning "After the blessing that followed the meal, the grandfather bought a religious book." In this simple sentence, the word *seyfer* comes from Hebrew, *bentshn* is of old Romance origin, the words *nokkn, hot, der*, and *gekoyft* are Germanic, and *zeyde* is Slavic.[6] The earliest speakers of Yiddish, most of whom came from Italy and other Romance-language countries, settled in Franco-German border regions. After Jews suffered a number of persecutions there during the Middle Ages, most of them migrated to Eastern Europe, taking their wandering language with them.

The new Viennese *Ostjuden*, whose habits were extremely conservative, were poor and worked in menial positions; for these reasons they were snubbed by the German-speaking Jews.[7] Jakob and Amalie are likely

---

[3] Among the many books on the role of Jews in fin-de-siècle Vienna, see Carl E. Schorske's *Fin-de-Siècle Vienna: Politics and Culture*, and Jacques Le Rider, *Modernité viennoise et crises de l'identité*.

[4] The word "ghetto," however, originally referred to the walled quarters where the segregated Jewish communities lived in major European cities. On the Leopoldstadt community, see Peter Gay, *Freud: A Life for Our Time*, p. 13.

[5] Whereas Hebrew was used as a literary and religious language, Yiddish was above all the language of everyday life, spoken particularly by women, who were not usually taught the sacred language. It was only after centuries had passed that a Yiddish literature arose, reaching its zenith with the advent of modern Jewish cultural movements. An extremely important part of modern Jewish culture is in Yiddish – for instance, Nobel laureate Isaac Bashevis Singer, wrote his fiction in Yiddish. See Guinsburg, *Aventuras de uma língua errante*, pp. 26-8.

[6] Weinrich, quoted in Ouaknin and Rotnemer, *La Bible de l'humour juif*, pp. 25-6.

[7] Gay, *Freud, Jews and Other Germans*, p. 185.

to have experienced some sort of discrimination when they went to live in the poorest working-class section of the Jewish district, where the Eastern Jewish population was concentrated. It was there that Freud grew up, living with his parents and siblings, until 1875, when the family moved to a more comfortable place.

It is not known when or how Freud's parents cast off Orthodox Judaism. It is clear, on the basis of the cap-in-the-mud episode Freud relates in *The Interpretation of Dreams* (1900), that Jakob Freud, of Hasidic background, was a devout Jew, at least when young: he himself says that on the Sabbath he dressed according to the religious prescriptions.[8] When he arrived in Vienna, he brought with him the *Tanakh* or family Hebrew Bible, with which he taught his children to read about the history of the Jewish people. It is also known that Jakob Freud continued reading the Book of Books to the very end of his life, and also preserved the habit of writing in the sacred language. Jakob gave the most gifted of his children the best Jewish education possible, given his means and the limitations of his day and age. In his Gymnasium years Freud studied the Tanakh and learned elementary Hebrew from Samuel Hammerschlag, who later became his personal friend. The gratitude he felt for his teacher was expressed in a short and simple text in which Freud acknowledges that Hammerschlag had the gift of teaching Jewish history without submitting it to nationalistic and dogmatic limitations.[9] So why did Freud write in a letter to Dwossis that his father had allowed him "to grow up in complete ignorance of everything that concerned Judaism"[10]? The statement is still puzzling; he may have intended to convey his lack of familiarity, during his upbringing, with strict adherence to ritual or mystical practices.

Instead, Amalie Freud took on the task of handing down the heritage of Judaism to her children through oral tradition: that is, speech and food. She organized all religious feasts, in which specific moments in Jewish history are celebrated by the preparation of special meals, as is common in every religion. Amalie spoke to her children solely in Yiddish, which Jews also call *mame loschen*, the mother tongue. Little Sigismund[11]

---

[8] Religious Jews must keep their heads covered at all times. Since the late eighteenth century, Jews who are not strictly orthodox, like Jakob Freud, restrict the practice to the Sabbath.

[9] See *SE*, vol. 7, p. 255. ["Contribuition; *Neue Freie Presse*: Obituary of Prof. Hammerchlag"]

[10] Letter from Freud to J. Dwossis, dated Dec. 15, 1930, quoted in Gay, *Freud, Jews*, p. 6.

[11] Jakob Freud registered his son in the family Bible as Sigismund Schlomo. Freud never

learned to express himself in this language. Later he collected a huge repertoire of Jewish jokes, usually told in Yiddish. *Jokes and Their Relation to the Unconscious* (1905) shows how familiar Freud is with Jewish ethical attitudes toward life, and how well he can use Yiddish to communicate within his ethnic group. Jewish humor expresses a sense of belonging without any religious or national affiliation.[12]

For Freud, jokes (*Witze*) reveal a particular talent of the Jewish people: the ability to laugh about themselves, and to appreciate the layers of possible meaning contained in the act of speech. Freud discovers in Jewish humor an aspect of the poetic function of language and the polyphony of voices it includes. *Witz* is related to *wissen*, a German verb meaning "to know"; Freud found that in jokes, as well as in dreams and in symptoms, a specific psychic activity of thinking is at work that does not correspond to the criteria of conscious thinking proper to the scientific tradition.

The *Witz*, seen by Freud himself as the most social of our psychical activities – in contrast with dreams or neurotic symptoms, which take place on the plane of fantasy – brings about a symbolic exchange that transforms a painful situation into a pleasurable experience. Philippe Lacoue-Labarthe and Jean-Luc Nancy suggest that the *Witz* was seen by Freud as a model of collective identification, and that it was the Jewish people that first provided him with a paradigm of this process.[13]

Even though Jakob and Amalie had left behind some of their orthodox religious practices and embraced the Enlightenment ideals then current in Europe, they did not hesitate to circumcise Sigismund. As noted in the family Bible, this rite took place on May 13, 1856, on the traditional eighth day after birth, marking the newborn child's inclusion in the Jewish community. Freud's parents clearly desired to perpetuate the transmission of the law and history of the Jewish people.

According to Daniel Boyarin, the physical act of marking the male reproductive organ "represents the genealogical claim for concrete histor-

---

used Schlomo, his paternal grandfather's name, and began using Sigmund in his signature in his last school years, officially adopting the name soon after he entered the university. As Gay observes, Freud never explained why he shortened his given name, so that any conjecture on the significance of this move can only be sheer speculation. See Gay, *Freud, Jews*, pp. 4-5.

[12] Martin S. Bergman, "Moses and the Evolution of Freud's Identity," in Ostow (ed.), *Judaism and Psychoanalysis*, p. 111.

[13] Lacoue-Labarthe and Nancy, "Le peuple juif ne rêve pas," in Colloque de Montpellier, *La Psychanalyse est-elle une histoire juive?*, p. 60.

ical memory as constitutive of Israel."[14] The *brith milah*, or *circumcision covenant*, like every other Biblical covenant, has a separating function, for it establishes a cut that marks absence or deprivation as capable of producing meaning. A privative practice, a sort of sculpture on the body itself, circumcision is a form of writing whose function is equivalent to a document of transmission,[15] a place of knowledge of the effects of symbolic power. Circumcision is a reminder that man is not simply a child of the flesh, but also of the symbolic: it is a sort of second birth, which removes the child from the natural world.

In his correspondence with Eduard Silberstein, his best friend during adolescence, Freud shows how he absorbed some of the signifiers of Jewish culture that had been handed down to him. In a light-hearted letter in which he comments on the gastronomic rituals of Jewish religious festivals, he lets us know that at his own home the Jewish New Year, Yom Kippur, Pesach, and Purim were always celebrated.

"Thus the Passover has a constipating effect due to unleavened bread and hardboiled eggs. Yom Kippur is so lugubrious a day not so much through God's wrath as through the plum jam and the evacuation it stimulates."[16]

The basic elements of the continuity of a cultural and religious tradition include the transmission of a body of living experiences, independently of direct communication and education. For instance, the young Sigismund was never to forget his mother's illustration of the Biblical "Dust thou art, and unto dust shalt thou return" (Gen. 3:19). Amalie Freud, realizing that her son found it difficult to accept what she was trying to tell him, rubbed the palms of her hands together, producing some dark scales of skin as samples of earth, in order to make our earthly lot vivid to her son. Dumbfounded, the boy was led to resign himself to the common human fate; he was to say later, in *The Interpretation of Dreams*, that he had learned quite early from his mother something about the inevitability of death.[17]

---

[14] Boyarin, *Carnal Israel: Reading Sex in Talmudic Culture*, p. 233.

[15] See Michel de Certeau, *The Writing of History*, p. 340.

[16] Freud to Silberstein, Sept. 18, 1874, *The Letters of Sigmund Freud to Eduard Silberstein*. Freud's letter to Emile Fluss of March 17, 1873 (published in Théo Pfrimmer, *Freud lecteur de la Bible*, ch. 2) indicates that at his home Purim was celebrated in accordance with the tradition spelled out in the Book of Ruth. Purim is a celebration of the Jewish people's deliverance from Haman, minister of Ahasuerus, King of Persia, who wished to destroy them. The Bible account is in the Book of Esther.

[17] See *SE*, vol. 4, p. 20. [*The Interpretation of Dreams*]

Though Freud was given a secular education, he was deeply familiar with Jewish ethics and outlooks. In a love letter he wrote to Martha Bernays, his wife-to-be, he makes it clear that it was not necessary for him to have studied in a Jewish school or attended the synagogue to arrive at the conclusion that "even if the form wherein the old Jews were happy no longer offers us any shelter, something of the core, of the essence of this meaningful and life-affirming Judaism [will] not be absent from our home."[18] This seems to suggest that Freud not only acknowledged being a part of the Jewish people but also treasured something in Judaism quite aside from the religion of his fathers and from any national identity. In these lines written to Martha he plainly asserts that, although obedience to the rules and laws of the Jewish religion no longer makes sense in his life, he still hopes to create and nourish his own, subjective version of the Jewish heritage, beyond any form of religious belief.

Freud's birth in the German-speaking Diaspora in the mid-nineteenth century, at a time when practically all aspects of social life and ideas were undergoing transformation, in one way or another must have provided a basis for the "prophecy" that a wandering Viennese poet supposedly made in a Vienna park about the eldest child of Amalie and Jakob Freud: that some day little Sigismund would become a minister of state.[19] Such a prediction was reasonable because at that time Jews had already been fully emancipated; the ghettos had been opened, citizenship rights had been granted, and Jews had begun to participate in the various political, intellectual, and artistic movements and trends that mobilized Europe. The emancipation movement was a consequence of the generalized acceptance of Enlightenment ideas, whose paramount political expression, liberalism, allowed the Jewish community to move out of the ghettos and the shtetls.

In Austria the movement came rather late in comparison with most other European countries; it was only in 1848 that Jews achieved complete emancipation – which, incidentally, would be taken away from them for a long period soon after. It was only with the triumph of political liberalism in 1867 that Jews could profit from full equality of civil rights. But the attainment of citizenship and the enthusiastic acceptance of the changes proposed by the emancipation movement was not a process that

---

[18] July 23, 1882. In *Letters of Sigmund Freud*, ed. Ernst L. Freud.
[19] Freud himself tells the story in *SE*, vol. 4, pp. 192-3. [*The Interpretation of Dreams*]

took place in linear fashion or without any sacrifices. For Jews had to face a strong resistance put up by Germanic liberal culture, which continued to stigmatize them on the basis of a number of prejudices that had taken hold of the Western imagination since the Middle Ages.

When one examines the works of many German-language writers of the nineteenth century, as Steven Beller observes in *Vienna and the Jews*, it becomes clear how much they were responsible for perpetuating the stereotype of the Jew that had been fabricated by the Holy See in the Middle Ages, as a degraded, filthy, pestilent creature. Ideally, the new citizens should give up every trace of their Jewish identity in order to become "good Jews," that is, Germanized Jews. These ideas were permeated with the prejudiced notion that Jews must be humanized or cured, an idea in turn inspired by pseudoscientific notions of Jewish "degeneracy." Indeed, this view of the Jews as a race was prevalent throughout Europe. Jean-Martin Charcot, under whom Freud studied in Paris in the 1890s, may be considered one of its defenders. He believed that "nervous diseases of all kinds are incomparably more frequent among Jews."[20]

In *Freud, Race, and Gender*, Sander Gilman carefully analyzes turn-of-the-century biological science and finds in it a scientism marked by the era's strong race-conscious slant, which labeled Jews as inferior and diseased. A central component of Gilman's reflection has to do with his research on the European mentality of the period, which insisted on seeing the Jews as a "race" of intrinsically pathological and sexually degenerate beings, especially prone to syphilis, madness, and certain types of cancer. The racial discourse[21] adopted by part of late-nineteenth-century science is of the utmost relevance to Gilman's conclusions as he grapples with the difficult issue of the Jewishness of psychoanalysis on the basis of its determining historical and conceptual aspects. According to Gilman, Jewish "degeneracy," treated in psychiatric textbooks as an unquestionable fact, was related to the theme of the body of the Jew (and the question of cir-

---

[20] Charcot, quoted in Le Rider, *Modernité viennoise*, p. 296.
[21] Kwame Anthony Appiah wrote *In My Father's House: Africa in the Philosophy of Culture* to show that human races exist only in the sphere of the ideas, concepts, and simplistic suppositions that tend to accompany their practical application, and that their field is limited even in biology. The notion of "race" underlying the forms of racism that proliferated in the first decades of the twentieth century is, however, according to Appiah, highly significant. During World War II racial categories grew to such an extent that Jewishness came to be seen in racial terms. Consequently the struggle against racism necessarily implied acceptance of these very same categories.

cumcision). Taking as his point of departure fundamental historical and cultural aspects, Gilman holds that "the form taken by the sexual in Freud's arguments, and the rhetoric used, were shaped by a number of factors, including the discourse about Jewish sexual anatomy and sexual identity."[22] Gilman's research shows that in Freud's Austria the Jew had become a category of exclusion: it defined what the Aryan was *not*.

For all the difficulties and disappointments that came along with emancipation, toward the end of the nineteenth century German-Jewish culture was seen by many as a new golden age in the Western world. If Jews were not fully represented in public office and positions of eminence in public administration, for several generations Jews made up a sort of "subgroup" in the sphere of culture in German and Austrian societies. In *Redemption and Utopia*, analyzing the links between religion and politics, Michel Löwy emphasizes that the trajectory followed by German-speaking Jewish intellectuals in *Mitteleuropa*[23] before World War II led to a new social category: the "Jewish intelligentsia." For generations this intelligentsia became responsible for a cultural flowering that gave the world the priceless works of Heine, Marx, Freud, Kafka, Benjamin, Einstein, and Schnitzler.[24] Thanks to the emancipation of Jews, all of these works and many others were able to benefit from two cultures, the German and the Jewish, and to plant in a fertile but fragile soil an immense cultural garden, which shortly thereafter was cruelly destroyed by Nazism.

What factors favored the rise of the Jewish intelligentsia? Which elements of the Jewish cultural tradition encouraged the emergence of several generations of Jewish intellectuals and artists, whom Nazi ideology eventually credited with the creation of modernism? What could be the common element between age-old Judaism and the modern avant-garde, which was often branded as "foreign" because it lacked nationalist elements and was said by Hitler to be driven by the "Jewish element"?[25]

Obviously, the successive generations of Jewish artists and intellectuals did not come out of the blue, or arise in the mythic tranquility of

---

[22] Gilman, *Freud, Race, and Gender*, p. 4.

[23] *Mitteleuropa* (German for "Central Europe") refers, in the nineteenth and early twentieth centuries, to a region historically unified by German culture: Germany and the Austro-Hungarian Empire with all its dependencies.

[24] See the Introduction of Löwy, *Redemption and Utopia*.

[25] For a study of the association between modern avant-garde movements and the "Jewish element," see Frederick Karl, *Modern and Modernism: The Sovereignty of the Artist, 1885-1925*.

the spirit; on the contrary, the phenomenon was shaped by historical, economic, and social conditions, which each individual was able (or unable) to profit from subjectively. From a socioeconomic point of view, the Jewish family structure, in a society that for thousands of years has been centered on values based on knowledge of Scripture, is seen by most historians and sociologists as the most important factor that triggered the rise of the generations of intellectuals after the advent of the Enlightenment.[26] In contrast with the Catholic majority, who lived in the country and whose children were put to use in farm work, German-speaking Jewish families tended to place their children in urban jobs in which professional success depended on more specialized education. Historically, the children of Jewish businessmen were largely responsible for the dynamism of turn-of-the-century Vienna. The logic of cultural assimilation and the desire to ascend socially led the Jewish bourgeoisie to send their children to university, which in the nineteenth century was the royal road to respectability, honor and social mobility. Clearly, not everyone in the Jewish population was involved in the changes made possible by emancipation. A large number of Jews were denied access to any knowledge other than the dogmas of religion; this was true particularly of that part of the population that was little given to book reading, being semi-illiterate and remote from the changes affecting Western culture. Freud's letters to his fiancée show clearly that in Vienna, where so many Jews lived worldly and intellectual lives, a large number of Jewish families remained strictly faithful to the traditional orthodoxy and had no interest in a secular education.[27] In any case, that Freud belonged to that part of the Jewish population which had left the ghetto and tried to enter the wider European society, embracing a new way of expressing Jewishness, is a fact that cannot be contested, not even by those who insist that Freud refused to accept his own Jewishness or did so only with great difficulty.[28]

As to the economic and social factors that drove Jews to the universities in Vienna, there is good reason to suppose that it was in the cultural and religious tradition of Judaism that this process found support. Twenty centuries earlier, in the year 70 B.C., seeing that the Temple had

---

[26] See Shmuel Trigano, *La Societé juive à travers l'histoire*, p. 438.

[27] Freud to Martha Bernays, Sept. 16, 1883, in *Letters of Sigmund Freud*.

[28] On Freud's attitudes of refusal or conflict in relation to Judaism, see the analyses of Le Rider, *Modernité viennoise* (chapter 4), Schorske, *Fin-de-Siècle Vienna* (chapter 4).

been destroyed and the Jews expelled from Jerusalem, Rabbi Jochanaan ben Zakkai advised all to continue to observe Mosaic Law wherever they might be, worshiping God, particularly on an individual basis, through the reading and interpretation of Scripture. Now that the Temple was no more, worship was to take place in the synagogue (*Schul*, or school), in which a school began to function, the rabbi's place in it being above all that of teacher of Scripture. The importance of this historical moment for the construction of the Jewish people's cultural and ethical heritage has not gone unnoticed. The German-Jewish poet Heinrich Heine, for one, used to say that the Bible was the Jewish people's "portable homeland," meaning that the entire community recognized the Book of Books as the sole authority to be followed in exile. It was in exile that laws were instituted enforcing study of the Sacred Texts, to make up for the loss of the Temple and to guarantee that the Jewish heritage would be handed down to future generations. These laws, most of them enshrined in the *Book of Principles* (*Pirkei Avot*), must be obeyed by all means, whatever costs or sacrifices they might imply. They gave rise to a tradition and a myth: to allow a son to study the Holy Books and in this way to ensure their transmission became a blessing. The entire Jewish religious tradition came to center on this obligation to preserve, on a solid and perpetual basis, the link between the different generations of the Jewish people scattered throughout the world.

Beginning in the Middle Ages, the figure of the *talmid chacham* (religious scholar) or Talmudist (interpreter of the Tanakh) gained importance: a man who became noted for his profound knowledge of the Torah. The Talmudist dedicated his entire life to the single purpose of studying the Book of Books and other sacred works, and came to occupy the place of guardian of the community's spiritual and cultural life. Talmudists then developed a unique practice of endless reading and writing of the Text, a practice that assumes that whatever is said or written may be said or written in a number of possible ways, none of which implies the exclusion of the others. The work of continuous retranscription of the letter – which, in its material and concrete incarnation as language, re-creates the world, like the divine breath – makes reading-writing not only the backbone of Jewish culture but also a model of transmission. And it was the testimony of transmission that brought the *talmid chacham* to embody the ideal that every Jew should become an impassioned and believing student of the letters of Scripture.

"Jewish Science": Genesis of a Prejudice

As a consequence of a process of assimilation and emancipation Talmudists progressively disappeared in the modern age and the figure of the Jewish intellectual, a product of the Enlightenment, gained importance. The result of this was the birth of a pariah [29] intelligentsia – nonconformist and revolutionary. In the mid-nineteenth century, the Jewish intellectual elite began to take progressive social and political stances. The mark of a Jewish intellectual was the affirmation of secularism, although sometimes traces of the religious tradition may be detected in several works by Jewish thinkers and writers.[30]

Generally speaking, the effects of the Enlightenment penetrated the Jewish community through the *Haskalah*, which advocated reform of traditional customs and religious dogmatism, and attempted to make religion and secular knowledge compatible. With the advent of emancipation, the logic of cultural assimilation became stronger: the vast majority of university-educated Jews gave up the tradition of reading the Torah, turning instead to cosmopolitan pursuits. Families were assimilated to such an extent that many of them were entirely shut off from tradition, at least consciously. These breaks necessarily brought about a number of crises and raised problems of communication between those Jews who kept up the tradition and those who desired to assimilate.[31]

Having moved away from orthodoxy, the Jewish intelligentsia delved into the classic texts of German literature and philosophy – Goethe

---

[29] See Hannah Arendt, *The Jew as Pariah: Jewish Identity and Politics in the Modern Age*. The notion of pariah appears in several of Arendt's books. In *The Origins of Totalitarianism* she shows how the making of a totalitarian society begins with the notion of the pariah and thus with the "exception." Arendt extends this concept of the Jewish paradigm to the thousands of "stateless persons," the better to understand prejudice when elevated to the status of an ideological weapon.

[30] For further details, see Löwy, *Redemption and Utopia*. Integrating different senses of the concept of "elective affinity," the author attempts to demonstrate how the thoughts and writings of various Jewish authors – Franz Kafka, Walter Benjamin, Martin Buber, Erich Fromm, György Lukács and others – were strongly marked both by German Romanticism and by Jewish Messianism.

[31] In *Modernité viennoise*, his study of the major figures of the Other in Viennese modernity, Le Rider shows that Jews found it necessary to devise strategies to restore their own universe, marked in late-nineteenth-century Central Europe by the achievements of emancipation, the advances in assimilation, and the wounds opened by the rise of anti-Semitism and contemporary nationalistic movements.

and Schiller, Kant and Hegel – with the same passion their ancestors had dedicated to the study of the Sacred Books. Most students entered the universities "as though they had been preparing for the entrance examinations for a thousand years."[32] The prodigal sons of Judaism, they almost invariably abandoned the religion of their fathers and became, to paraphrase Löwy, disarmed prophets, for the book and the pen were their only weapons.[33] The Trotskyite philosopher Isaac Deutscher, who had been a Talmudist as a young man, wrote in his essay "The Non-Jewish Jew" that for several generations intellectuals of Jewish origin shared a deep-seated contempt for nationalistic or religious ideas. These iconoclastic and agnostic Jewish intellectuals, who excluded themselves from the community, were attuned to the universal to the point of becoming, according to Deutscher, "non-Jewish."

Undoubtedly, their cultural tradition and experience gave them a foothold in the new world that now opened for them. But in contrast with the Torah scholar, who could count on immediate acknowledgment by his community, the modern Jewish intellectual had to seek work outside the ghetto, in a world where the criteria for acceptance and recognition were quite different. In European society, the social organization made upward mobility harder for everyone, and the newly enfranchised citizens were confronted with a different competitive structure and an inevitable political struggle.[34] It was always more difficult for a Jew to be heard and respected in a society that, even though it had granted him the right of citizenship, still treated him as a foreigner in spite of the fact that he had been born and raised in his own country. And so it was that Freud had to wait for seventeen years until he was appointed professor at Vienna's Faculty of Medicine. In the Austria of his time a rule was in force – the *numerus clausus* – that limited the number of Jewish professors to two percent of the faculty.

Those were stressful years for German and Austrian Jews, when latent anti-Semitism cast a shadow on the prospects opened by the Enlightenment, forcing them to see how deceptive was the promise of equality held out by assimilation, as Arendt points out throughout her works. This is borne out by Heine, who observed that conversion to Christianity was the "entrance-ticket to European society."[35] Heine's aphorism aptly sum-

---

[32] Frederic V. Grunfeld, *Prophets Without Honour*, pp. 1-2.
[33] Löwy, *Redemption and Utopia*, Introduction.
[34] Trigano, *Société juive*, p. 241.
[35] Quoted in Paul Johnson, *History of the Jews*, p. 310.

marizes the situation of Jews, who were still discriminated against even though they were forced to accept social responsibilities ever since emancipation began. The fact remains that, within German and Austrian societies, the issue of Jewishness was an ever-present preoccupation for Jewish intellectuals.[36]

As Enzo Traverso observes in his study of Jewish intellectuals and German culture, for several generations – and independently of individual choices – these men, whether religious or atheistic, whether Zionists or internationalists, were all divided between cultural assimilation and the sort of social ghetto with invisible boundaries that forced them to reconsider the issue of "being Jewish." This issue was always somehow present in the elaboration of their works, which eventually came to permeate the entire culture of the Austrian capital.

In the long and painful social history of the assimilation and emancipation of German-speaking Jewish intellectuals, different stands were taken vis-à-vis the endless task of translating the mark each one of them carried. If to some it was a curse to be the majority's Other, to Freud being a member of the Jewish people was, since his childhood, a positive experience, the promise of a glorious future. In *The Interpretation of Dreams* he tells us that at the time of the liberal government of Vienna that established the Austrian Constitution of 1867, "every industrious Jewish schoolboy carried a Cabinet Minister's portfolio in his satchel."[37] This meant that there was always a hope, almost utopian, of being able to swim against the current of latent anti-Semitism and join in the creation of a new "promised land."

Even when he was badly shaken and pained by aggressive anti-Semitism – "When, in 1873, I first joined the University, I experienced some appreciable disappointments. Above all, I found that I was expected to feel myself inferior and an alien because I was a Jew" – Freud never let

---

[36] See Arendt, *Rahel Varnhagen: The Life of a Jewess*. To appreciate the fact that the Jewish struggle for assimilation continued into the next generation, it is worth mentioning Einstein's testimony. When he arrived in Berlin in 1929 to continue with his studies, confronted with the shocking fact of Nazi propaganda, he declared: "When I came to Germany... I discovered for the first time that I was a Jew, and I owe this discovery more to Gentiles than Jews." These words clearly sum up one of the conundrums in the difficult process of assimilation and emancipation: even when a Jew identified totally with European culture and did not consider himself a Jew at all, it was still difficult for him to evade the issues raised by the circumstances of his birth.

[37] *SE*, vol. 4, p. 193. [*The Interpretation of Dreams*]

himself be intimidated. He decided to face the aggressions and disadvantages imposed by European society by positively asserting his condition as a Jew: "I have never been able to see why I should feel ashamed of my descent or, as people were beginning to say, of my 'race.' I put up, without much regret, with my non-acceptance in the community; for it seemed to me that in spite of this exclusion an active fellow-worker could not fail to find some nook or cranny in the framework of humanity."[38]

In response to the discriminations he suffered, Freud learned to live "in Opposition to the compact majority"; because of this "the foundations were... laid for a certain degree of independence of judgment." Isolation ultimately had the effect of reinforcing the young Freud's practice of thinking independently, which, as Arendt has observed, is precisely what gives the subject the possibility of shedding prejudices.[39]

In this "glorious heroic age," Freud later wrote, "like Robinson Crusoe, I settled down as comfortably as possible on my desert island."[40] Psychoanalysis was definitely "not Jewish, nor Catholic, nor pagan,"[41] for science should overstep all boundaries of national identity: "there should be no such thing as a specifically Aryan science or Jewish science. These results should be identical, only the presentation might change.... If the differences extend into the interpretation of the objective data of science, it must be because something is not right."[42]

How did Freud struggle to assert his uniqueness and allow psychoanalysis to be acknowledged, rather than attacked, by Jews and non-Jews? What strategies did he rely on to face the countless obstacles and resistances that opposed his discovery from the very beginning?

In contrast to the thinking of the masses, Freud subverted the belief in dogmatic adherence to common truths and promoted the listening to the subjective truth expressed by the formations of the unconscious, including the unconscious grounds for resistances. When Max Graf, father of "Little Hans", asked him whether he should baptize his son in order to protect his family from anti-Semitism, he replied: "If you do not let your son grow up as a Jew, you will deprive him of those sources of energy

---

[38] *SE*, vol. 20, p. 9. [*An Autobiographical Study*]

[39] Arendt, *Rahel Varnhagen*, p. 90.

[40] *SE*, vol. 14, p. 22. ["On the History of the Psycho-Analytic Movement"]

[41] Quoted in Le Rider, *Modernité viennoise*, p. 285.

[42] Unpublished letter from Freud to Sandor Ferenczi, dated June 8, 1913, quoted in the Introduction of Jacques Chemouni, *Freud et le sionisme*.

which cannot be replaced by anything else. He will have to struggle as a Jew, and you ought to develop in him all the energy that he will need for that struggle."[43]

There is an obvious homology between this observation and the advice that Freud gave analysts throughout his work, to struggle against all resistances to the analytic process, beginning with inner resistances. *"Everything which destroys the continuation of the work is a resistance."*[44] Freud acknowledged the existence of resistances as a present and constant force in analysis. This led him to request that each analyst submit himself to the process of analysis, to the listening of the discourse of the unconscious, of the Other.

Freud faced two major resistances outside the theoretical-clinical sphere: that of the dominant medical culture against his discoveries and that of a society increasingly drawn to aggressive anti-Semitic propaganda. The struggle for the recognition of psychoanalysis and for a way of being Jewish that Freud himself had invented implied facing resistances, tapping inner "energy sources" in order to "struggle" against them, and learning to turn resistance into an "advantage."

At the dawn of the twentieth century, even as Jews were being described as inferior human beings, psychoanalysis was labeled a byproduct of Viennese culture – Vienna being seen as a city where customs were excessively flexible and liberal. Freud himself pointed to the connection between the two criticisms: "the reproach of being a citizen of Vienna is only a euphemistic substitute for another reproach which no one would care to put forward openly"[45] – namely, that of being Jewish.[46]

---

[43] Quoted in Yerushalmi, *Freud's Moses: Judaism Terminable and Interminable*, p. 14.

[44] Jacques Lacan, *Freud's Papers on Technique*, p. 33. [Le Séminaire, livre I, *Les écrits techniques de Freud*, III, "La résistance et les défenses," pp. 43-44.]

[45] *SE*, vol. 14, pp. 53-4. ["On The History of the Psycho-Analytic Movement"]

[46] If we consider the early history of psychoanalysis, following Freud's account, as the history of the resistance to the idea that sex drives cannot be entirely domesticated, this resistance implies a form of age-old prejudice against sex and against Jews. Saint Augustine himself had made the accusation in his *Tractatus adversus Judaeos*: *"Behold Israel according to the flesh"* [1 Cor. 10:18]. This we know to be the carnal Israel; but the Jews do not grasp this meaning and as a result they prove themselves indisputably carnal." Quoted in Boyarin, *Carnal Israel*, p. 1. In this book Boyarin interprets sex in Judaism and the difference that arose between Jews and Christians over their views on the body and the spirit.

Betty B. Fuks

Rome-Canaan: On Isolation, Endurance, and Determination

The social and historical universe that made it possible for psychoanalytic discourse to arise encompasses the vicissitudes of the Jew's fate in the West. The political drama in which Vienna's Jews lived at the time of the inception of psychoanalysis emerged in several of the dreams Freud discusses in *The Interpretation of Dreams*. His so-called Roman dreams[47] are particularly interesting for our purposes, for they are related to a childhood memory that will allow us to develop some ideas further:

> I may have been ten or twelve years old, when my father began to take me with him on his walks and reveal to me in his talk his views upon things in the world we live in. Thus it was, on one such occasion, that he told me a story to show me how much better things were now than they had been in his days. 'When I was a young man,' he said, 'I went for a walk one Saturday in the streets of your birthplace; I was well dressed, and had a new fur cap on my head. A Christian came up to me and with a single blow knocked off my cap into the mud and shouted: "Jew! get off the pavement!"' 'And what did you do?' I asked. 'I went into the roadway and picked up my cap,' was his quiet reply. This struck me as unheroic conduct on the part of the big, strong man who was holding the little boy by the hand.[48]

In his comment on this childhood memory, associated with his four dreams of Rome, Freud says he could not forgive his father for the resignation with which he reacted to such an insult. When he was told about this episode he swore to avenge his father some day. In the countless readings by psychoanalysts and even by historians of culture who attempt to explain psychoanalysis as the product of Freud's effort to overcome the humiliation experienced by his father, Freud has often been "psychoana-

---

[47] Freud's dreams have been exhaustively analyzed in psychoanalytic literature and in studies of the Jewish question in Freud. The following pages will center on the four Roman dreams and the childhood memories associated with them. The other dreams in which the Jewish question is evident are the following: "close the eyes/an eye," which manifests the conflict between respect for tradition and assimilation; the "uncle with the yellow beard" dream, in which Freud wonders how he and his children might be spared anti-Semitism; and "my son the Myops," inspired by a play by Theodor Herzl, the founder of Zionism, about a Jewish father concerned with the future of his children, to whom he cannot give a fatherland.

[48] *SE*, vol. 4, p. 197. [*The Interpretation of Dreams*]

lyzed" on the strength of this episode.[49] As Freud himself stated, *The Interpretation of Dreams* had a strongly subjective meaning for him: it was when his father died that he finally embarked on the task of discovering the unconscious through his dreams, self-analysis, and in correspondence with Fliess.

Freud's acknowledgment of the importance of this moment in his life for the progress of his work may have stoked the imagination of a number of authors, who cannot resist the temptation of psychoanalyzing the creator of psychoanalysis. We will try to trace the interpretations he made of his memories of the "cap-in-the-mud" on the basis of his analysis of his Roman dreams.

Rome is merely glimpsed from a distance in the first of the four Roman dreams: "I dreamt once that I was looking out of a railway-carriage window at the Tiber and the Ponte Sant'Angelo. The train began to move off, and it occurred to me that I had not so much as set foot in the city."[50] Freud does not attempt to analyze this dream, but simply leaves the reader faced with his inability to enter the city he longed to visit.

Commenting on this dream in *Freud's Self-Analysis*, Didier Anzieu observes that just beyond the Tiber and the Ponte Sant'Angelo lies the Vatican, the seat of Catholic power, which persecuted the Jews. Thus the Rome appearing in Freud's first dream evoked for him Western anti-Semitism, the beginnings of which are symbolically if not historically associated with the creation of the Holy See. Freud, who was well versed in the history of the Catholic Church and patristic philosophy, developed intensely ambivalent feelings for the Eternal City, without ever disguising his affection for it. Thus, on his fifth trip to Italy, Freud finally fulfilled his wish to visit Rome, but he was not able to enjoy fully the occasion he had been anticipating for such a long time. A sort of specter haunted him in the cradle of European civilization: "But, while I contemplated ancient Rome undisturbed... I found I could not freely enjoy the second [i.e., medieval, Christian] Rome."[51]

---

[49] Many attempts to psychoanalyze Freud have been made since the beginning of psychoanalysis. The earliest, according to Yerushalmi, was undertaken by Charles Maylan, in *Freuds tragischer Komplex*. According to Maylan, psychoanalysis is a product of the age-old humiliation and desire for revenge of a typically disagreeable race. The cap-in-the-mud incident is discussed in his book in a chapter titled "The Jew in the Excrement." Freud's identification with Hannibal is said to express his desire to avenge the humiliations suffered by his father and to undermine Christianity, replacing the Roman papacy with an international papacy of Reason. See Yerushalmi, *Freud's Moses*, pp. 58-9.

[50] *SE*, vol. 4, pp. 193-94. [*The Interpretation of Dreams*]

[51] Freud, *The Origins of Psycho-Analysis*, letter of Sept. 19, 1901, p. 335.

In opposition to the Christian Rome he feared and could not identify with, Freud built another Rome, familiar and desired, and in his second dream was able to fulfill his longing to "see the promised land from afar": "Another time someone led me to the top of a hill and showed me Rome half-shrouded in mist; it was so far away that I was surprised at my view of it being so clear. There was more in the content of this dream than I feel prepared to detail; but the theme of 'the promised land seen from afar' was obvious in it."[52]

In opposition to those authors who insist on reading this dream as no more than Freud's identification with the Biblical figure of Moses, whom YHWH drove to the top of the mountain of Nebo to show him the Promised Land from afar, I would emphasize that the contents of a dream transcend imaginary identifications. Could it be that by merging the Christian city with the Promised Land Freud was attempting to establish proximity between two terms seen as a disjunction – to enter the Eternal City with no fear of forgetting Jerusalem?

> If I forget thee, O Jerusalem,
> let my right hand forget her cunning.
> If I do not remember thee,
> let my tongue cleave to the roof of my mouth;
> if I prefer not Jerusalem
> above my chief joy. (Psalm 137)

To merge cities that are opposed to each other and separate in time and space is to fulfill a wish, in accordance with his theory of dreams: the desire to think the unthinkable, the unsayable, the invisible. The appearance of the signifier *Rome-Canaan*[53] as the effect of the dream logic is in itself so revealing that no interpretation is necessary. *Rome-Canaan* transforms Rome *and* Canaan into Rome *is* Canaan.

The same logic is implied in Freud's third Roman dream. If it is indeed true that all roads lead to Rome, Freud chose the one that was most familiar to him: two Jewish jokes concerning the sociopolitical reality of Jews in the modern world are the underlying remnants of the day. "*I noticed a Herr Zucker whom I knew slightly and determined to ask him the way to the city.*"[54]

---

[52] *SE*, vol. 4, pp. 193-94. [*The Interpretation of Dreams*]

[53] The signifier *Rome-Canaan* was coined by Marthe Robert in her analysis of the Roman dreams. See Robert, *D'Œdipe à Moïse*.

[54] *SE*, vol. 4, pp. 193-94. [*The Interpretation of Dreams*]

Zucker (whose name means "sugar") is an unsuccessful Jew, a schlemiel, trying to travel without a ticket on the express train to Karlsbad, a spa to which sufferers of diabetes were often referred early in the century. But the stowaway is immediately caught: at the first stop he is kicked off the train. This situation is repeated again and again, for the man will not give up his intent. At one stop in his *via dolorosa* the stowaway meets an acquaintance who, surprised to see him in that state, asks him where he is going. Weary and breathless, he gives a surprising reply: "To Karlsbad, if my constitution can stand it."

The complexity of the presence of the Jew in a space that was both outside and inside the host nation is emphasized in this *Witz*: Emancipated, but exiled in the everyday life of Europe, the Jew was torn between the break with tradition and the desire to explore what is unknown in the city, to penetrate the invisibility of Rome. The meaning we would like to attach to this joke, which eloquently expresses the vicissitudes of Jews' fate in the nineteenth century, is somewhat analogous to the meaning Freud reads into his dreams: the desire to go to Rome overlies a number of desires, and to achieve them he would have to struggle with determination and resistance.[55]

The other joke associated with the third dream also involves the adventures of a schlemiel: a Jew who is going to Paris is advised by a malicious friend to ask the way to the famous Rue Richelieu. The point of the joke is that, since the final vowel sound of "Richelieu" does not exist in Yiddish, in attempting to pronounce it the poor Jew will immediately betray his Jewish origin in a foreign country. Unaware of this trap, when he arrives in Paris the Jew asks the question of a passerby who, though apparently a Frenchman like any other, is in fact a successful fellow Jew. In perfect French he explains how to get to Rue Richelieu. But the schlemiel notices a very slight accent in the other, and reacting indignantly to what he takes to be an imposture, replies in Yiddish: "You and I both know what is needed for the preparation of the Sabbath, for we are both Jews."[56]

The first joke has to do with the lies of emancipation and of contemporary Jews' difficulties of assimilation; the second joke depicts with-

---

[55] Ibid., p. 197. [*The Interpretation of Dreams*]

[56] Freud makes only a passing mention to this second joke, but thanks to Didier Anzieu's research, in chapter 3 of his *Freud's Self-Analysis*, we now know the entire joke in its original form. Anzieu's analysis also emphasizes the meaning of the name "Richelieu," which combines the French words for "rich" and "place": the attraction to profit, another trait commonly attributed to Jews.

out any condescension the inner crisis among Jews at a time of change. Although the notion that Jews are the chosen people implies that all the descendants of Abraham are equal before the law,[57] crises nevertheless occurred within the community. Those who were rich or who had book knowledge enjoyed concrete advantages over the rest. But in the face of the common enemy – anti-Semitism – the rich and the poor, the wise and the ignorant were gradually driven to the same fate. Both jokes clearly expressed the idea that the Jew cannot escape the mark on him.

Freud chose neither to hide this mark nor simply to follow his parents' footsteps. His faithfulness to Judaism was part and parcel of a Jewishness practiced outside and inside the cultural heritage handed down by his forefathers. Indeed, Freud lived and worked in accordance with the idea that being a Jew was not an essence, but a movement – it meant wandering. Moving from Jerusalem to the Acropolis and to Rome, leaving Vienna for Paris or Berlin – this was Freud's way of wandering and overstepping the resistance of the West against the Jew in psychoanalysis. Paris was another object of Freud's desire. In the last years of the nineteenth century, he arrived there like the Jew in the jokes about the train and about the man with the Yiddish accent: poor, facing many difficulties, but filled with the desire to conquer the City of Light: "Paris itself had for many long years been another goal of my longings; and the blissful feelings with which I first set foot on its pavement seemed to me a guarantee that others of my wishes would be fulfilled as well."[58]

As soon as he arrived in Paris, Freud went to see the source of wealth on Rue Richelieu: "Today I walked... away from the Seine," he wrote to Martha. "I found myself surrounded by the most frantic Paris hubbub until I worked my way through to the well-known Boulevards and the Rue Richelieu."[59] It was on this street that he would find the Bibliothèque Nationale and the Comédie-Française. In Paris, the young man was able to earn the respect of the intelligentsia, to overcome the language barrier, and become his mentor Charcot's German translator.

It was in his fourth Roman dream that Freud revived the memory of the episode experienced by his father, who had his cap knocked into the mud. Freud sees himself wandering about the streets of Rome and is surprised to find a large number of posters in German on the walls. *Rome-*

---

[57] As Jacó Guinsburg observes, in his *Aventuras de uma língua errante*.
[58] *SE*, vol. 4, p. 195. [*The Interpretation of Dreams*]
[59] *Letters of Sigmund Freud*, p. 174.

Berlin is the signifier that, according to Freud himself, expresses his desire to be in Rome with his dear Berlin friend Wilhelm Fliess. Freud had confided to Fliess that the deep anxiety the city of Rome inspired in him was associated with his boyhood infatuation with Hannibal[60] and the horror he had felt when he learned that his father had not reacted against insults. In contrast to his father's perceived lack of heroism, the boy evoked a scene that was more consistent with his expectations and feelings: "the scene in which Hannibal's father, Hamilcar Barca, made his boy swear before the household altar to take vengeance on the Romans."[61]

The story of Hannibal was marked by this oath, which led him to become a great warrior. After a brilliant early career, he fell from military power, a fact that had serious consequences for his family: his brother Hasdrubal was killed by the Romans, who had quickly reorganized after losing the battles against Hannibal's army. When the Carthaginian general retreated in order to protect the threatened Carthage, he realized that defeat was imminent and committed suicide. So it was that Hamilcar's son became a failed hero. Freud admired him all the same: "Hannibal and Rome symbolized the conflict between the tenacity of Jewry and the organization of the Catholic Church."[62]

It is at this point of his analysis that Freud asks himself how to fulfill his wish to go to Rome, contraposing another figure to the warrior: "Which of the two, it may be debated, walked up and down his study with the greater impatience after he had formed his plan of going to Rome – Winckelmann, the Vice-Principal, or Hannibal, the Commander-in-Chief?"[63] Winckelmann, the archeologist and art historian, eventually converted to Catholicism so that he could occupy the post of librarian to the Pope: "It is the love of science and nothing else that may lead me to consider the proposal I have been made,"[64] Winckelmann argued when he decided to abandon his Protestant faith. Unlike the archaeologist, Freud says no to conversion. His struggle to overcome the effects of the discrimination he had to face because he occupied a marginal position in relation to the dominant culture will take place on a different level of events. In 1901 he finally visited the Rome he had dreamed of when he wrote *The*

---

[60] Freud, *The Origins of Psycho-Analysis*, letter of Dec. 3, 1987, p. 236.
[61] *SE*, vol. 4, p. 197. [*The Interpretation of Dreams*]
[62] Ibid., p. 196.
[63] Ibid.
[64] Quoted in Chapter IV of Robert, *D'Oedipe à Moïse*.

Interpretation of Dreams: his Jerusalem must remain present but invisible, always beyond the navel of the dream.

Between-the-Two: Anti-Chauvinism and Spiritual Alliances

Freud, who used to say of his discovery that he felt like "a Jewish father" for whom the "assurance that the children will be provided for... is a matter of life and death,"[65] soon started an anti-chauvinistic policy to avoid the danger of making the unconscious a refined cultural theme for fin-de-siècle Vienna or a national Jewish subject, which would thereby consign it to one ghetto or another. Thus everyone who joined the cause of psychoanalysis was immediately committed to the project of dissociating it from Vienna and the Jewish ghetto. The prime example of this is Freud's insistence on placing Carl Gustav Jung, a Swiss doctor, at the forefront of the movement, as he makes clear in his correspondence. In response to Abraham's suspicion of Jung's theoretical deviations, Freud wrote:

> Please be tolerant and do not forget that it is really easier for you than it is for Jung to follow my ideas, for in the first place you are completely independent, and then you are closer to my intellectual constitution because of racial kinship, while he as a Christian and a pastor's son finds his way to me only against great inner resistances. His association with us is the more valuable for that. I nearly said that it was only by his appearance on the scene that psycho-analysis escaped the danger of becoming a Jewish national affair.[66]

---

[65] *Letters of Sigmund Freud*, letter of July 9, 1913.

[66] Hilda Abraham and Ernst L. Freud (eds.), *A Psycho-analytic Dialogue*, letter of May 11, 1908. Until the creation of psychoanalysis, what Freud had in common with his closest interlocutors was the fact that they were all of Jewish origin: Samuel Hammerschlag, a friend who taught him about Judaism and helped to pay for his education; Josef Breuer, his partner in clinical practice, who had a major impact on his early training; and, finally, his close friend, Dr. Wilhelm Fliess, with whom he had an intense correspondence and an "analytic situation" that obviously was not acknowledged as such. Octave Mannoni stresses the fact that the deep friendship between these two men sustained the process of the "original analysis" (Freud's "self-analysis"). See Mannoni, *Freud*, p. 59.

What should be observed in this letter is that Freud's intention of expanding psychoanalysis outside the Jewish world coexists with his efforts to reinforce the alliance with his Jewish colleagues by emphasizing intellectual, cultural, and affective factors. This attempt to remain close to the Jewish community, it should be stressed, persisted as a way of resisting intolerable pressures. This is clearly what Freud had in mind when he wrote to Ferenczi at the time of the break with Jung: "You have heard that Jung had declared in America that psychoanalysis was not a science but a religion. That would certainly illuminate the whole difference. But there the Jewish spirit regretted not being able to join in."[67]

While Freud practiced no religion whatsoever it is clear that he asserted his own Jewishness, particularly when anti-Semitic attacks became common throughout Europe. In 1926 he stated: "My language is German. My culture, my attainments are German. I considered myself German intellectually, until I noticed the growth of anti-Semitic prejudice in Germany and German Austria. Since that time I prefer to call myself a Jew."[68] As to psychoanalysis, Freud wrote to Enrico Morselli that same year that he was not sure if it is "a direct product of the Jewish mind... but if it is I wouldn't be ashamed. Although I have been alienated from the religion of my forbears for a long time, I have never lost the feeling of solidarity with my people."[69]

Late in life, when he was aware of having superseded his own father,[70] Freud understood and accepted his father's strategy of endurance. In 1908 he wrote to Karl Abraham:

---

[67] Unpublished letter to Ferenczi, dated July 8, 1913, quoted in Chemouni, *op. cit.*

[68] From a 1926 interview with George Sylvester Vierk, quoted in http://www.bh.org.il/Exhibitions/Freud/freudbiog.asp (on April 1, 2004).

[69] *Letters of Sigmund Freud*, p. 365.

[70] In a 1939 letter to Romain Rolland, Freud speaks about a feeling of unease related to a trip to the Acropolis he had made with his brother Alexander in 1904. Freud says for many years he doubted the existence of the Acropolis because he thought he would never be able to visit it. The disturbance he experienced when he finally arrived there, according to his own interpretation, was an effect of his success in superseding his father, who, having no secondary education, knew nothing about Greek culture and was indifferent to Athens, one of the cradles of Western civilization. Freud's experience in the Acropolis is treated in psychoanalytic literature as a paradigm of the syndrome of failure brought about by success as evinced by one's superiority to one's father. See *SE.*, vol. 22, p. 237. ["A Disturbance of Memory on the Acropolis"]

I nurse a suspicion that the suppressed anti-Semitism of the Swiss that spares me is deflected in reinforced form upon you. But I think that we as Jews, if we wish to join in, must develop a bit of masochism, be ready to suffer some wrong. Otherwise there is no hitting it off. Rest assured that, if my name were Oberhuber, in spite of everything my innovations would have met with far less resistance.[71]

The strategic logic ("if we wish to join in") expressed in this letter, makes endurance not only a tactic of survival in time of struggle and war, but also the promise of affirmation and transmission. Freud persistently manifested solidarity with the Jewish cause. He deconstructed the meanings traditionally attributed to "Jew" and "Judaism" in the West in order to construct a Jewishness that made the invention of psychoanalysis possible. This may be his answer to the question he raised to the Swiss pastor Oskar Pfister: "…why was it that none of all the pious ever discovered psychoanalysis? Why did it have to wait for a completely godless Jew?"[72]

---

[71] Freud to Abraham, July 23, 1908, in *Complete Correspondence of Sigmund Freud and Karl Abraham*.
[72] Freud to Pfister, Oct. 9, 1918, in *Psycho-Analysis and Faith; The Letters of Sigmund Freud & Oskar Pfister*.

Chapter 2
Reading Freud, Psychoanalysis, and Judaism

> *A Jew is one who is crazy enough to admit he is a Jew. It's not in your blood or in your language.*
>
> AMOS OZ[1]

In the closing lines of "The Resistances to Psycho-Analysis" (1925) Freud makes a few observations that raise the question of the links between his Jewishness and the creation of psychoanalysis. He wonders whether his never having attempted

> to disguise the fact that he is a Jew may not have had a share in provoking the antipathy of his environment to psycho-analysis. An argument of this kind is not often uttered aloud. But we have unfortunately grown so suspicious that we cannot avoid thinking that this factor may not have been quite without its effect. Nor is it perhaps entirely a matter of chance that the first advocate of psycho-analysis was a Jew. To profess belief in this new theory called for a certain degree of readiness to accept a situation of solitary opposition – a situation with which no one is more familiar than a Jew.[2]

In asserting his Jewishness, Freud encourages analysts to endure the loneliness of the pioneers, the isolation that comes with the recognition of a difference that cannot be assimilated.

For many years – "since official science had pronounced its solemn ban upon psycho-analysis"[3] – Freud faced opposition to his discovery. His choice was also influenced by the political difficulties brought about by the rising tide of anti-Semitism in Austria. But as he observed in "On the History of the Psycho-Analytic Movement," if solitude had disadvantages, it also allowed him to experience a situation of separation from the world, a condition required by great discoveries.

---

[1] Interview in *O Globo*, Rio de Janeiro, June 3, 1994.
[2] *SE*, vol. 19, p. 222. ["The Resistances to Psycho-Analysis"]
[3] *SE*, vol. 14, pp. 43-4. ["On the History of the Psycho-Analytic Movement"]

The intimation that he was about to join those who "disturbed the sleep of the world"[4] led Freud to seek peers outside the field of medicine. In other spheres of learning, he hoped to find recognition of, and receptiveness to, his "unpleasing discoveries." As early as 1895 he joined the Vienna chapter of the B'nai B'rith (Sons of the Covenant), a Jewish cultural and philanthropic association modeled along the lines of the freemasonry. Founded in New York in 1834, it undertook an educational and humanitarian mission, based on secularism, cosmopolitanism, and faithfulness to the liberal tradition. Over many decades, Freud lectured to B'nai B'rith members on a number of occasions, and he regularly attended their fortnightly Tuesday meetings, which shows that he continually sought the company of Jews who were secular, liberal, and ethically concerned. Acknowledging the receptiveness he always found in the organization, he sent a message of gratitude to all its members, which was read in the meeting held to celebrate his seventieth birthday. This text, it should be noted, was written at roughly the same time as "The Resistances to Psycho-Analysis":

> the announcement of my unpleasing discoveries had as its result the severance of the greater part of my human contacts; I felt as though I were despised and universally shunned. In my loneliness I was seized with a longing to find a circle of picked men of high character who would receive me in a friendly spirit in spite of my temerity. Your society was pointed out to me as the place where such men were to be found.
> That you were Jews could only be agreeable to me; for I was myself a Jew, and it had always seemed to me not only unworthy but positively senseless to deny the fact. What bound me to Jewry was (I am ashamed to admit) neither faith nor national pride, for I have always been an unbeliever and was brought up without any religion though not without a respect for what are called the "ethical" standards of human civilization.... There was a perception that it was to my Jewish nature alone that I owed two characteristics that had become indispensable to me in the difficult course of my life. Because I was a Jew I found myself free from many prejudices which restrained others in the use of their intellect; and as a Jew I was prepared to join the Opposition and to do without agreement with the "compact majority."[5]

---

[4] Ibid., p. 21.
[5] *SE*, vol. 20, pp. 273-4. [Address to the Society of B'nai B'rith]

Freud demonstrates that "being" Jewish does not depend on blood or language, as the epigraph of this chapter asserts. The phrase "Jewish nature," as well as other phrases that Freud used in his letters to his Jewish colleagues – "Jewish spirit," "common race," and so on – take on a particularly rich meaning when they are seen in the context in which Freud found himself, that is, as belonging both to the Jewish people and to the German-speaking intelligentsia. Freud is perfectly aware of what he is saying: to refuse the "compact majority" meant, throughout his work and life, never coinciding with any whole. A man who always needed to experience differences, Freud kept a distance from all Jewish religious practices and separated himself from Viennese scientific culture, without ever ceasing to be a Jew and a scientist.

The condition of Jews as a separate minority in a society of equals dates back to the age-old Jewish exiles – the Babylonian exile in the sixth century B.C.E., the Roman exile, and finally the post-Roman exile – that made the Jews face the experience of the Diaspora. Diaspora means dispersion: "being dispersed among peoples," "being outside," or rather, "not belonging."[6] The very word contains the idea of the experience of rupture that touches upon the basic realities of the existence of the Jewish people. Maurice Blanchot inquires:

> "What does being Jewish signify? Why does it exist?" ... it exists so that the idea of exodus and the idea of exile can exist as a legitimate movement; it exists, through exile and through the initiative that is exodus, so that the experience of strangeness may affirm itself close at hand as an irreducible relation; it exists so that, by the authority of this experience, we might learn to speak.[7]

The subject of the Diaspora is born into a country in which he is both an insider and an outsider, one who occupies an intermediary position that allows him to share in the identity of the nation, but at the same time sustains "a piece" of himself elsewhere.[8]

From its very beginnings, psychoanalysis came to occupy a place in culture quite close to that of the Jewish people: always in movement, out-

---

[6] Rotker, Chocrón, and Lerner, *Los transgresores de la literatura venezolana*, p. 21.

[7] Blanchot, *The Infinite Conversation*, p. 125.

[8] Even after the creation of the state of Israel the concept of Diaspora remains alive in Jewish culture, because among the Jews scattered around the world the feeling of not-belonging lives on.

side the space of the majority. Freud's invention happens to inhabit a region "in between": in between science, art, philosophy, literature, religion, and myth.

The drive, the founding concept of psychoanalysis, is a concept that lies in between the psychic and the somatic, belonging neither to one domain nor to the other. In contrast to the instinct, a genetically acquired behavior, the drive reflects at once biological, psychological, and social foundations. It illustrates the number of fields encompassed by psychoanalysis and the "extraterritorial" nature of its knowledge.

"Psychoanalyzing" Freud and Judaism

"The present work," writes Jacques Le Rider in the chapter "The Culture of Modernity," "is indebted to psychoanalysis for some of its essential ideas, but it was not conceived as strictly... psychoanalytic. Freud the man will appear in it as often as Freudian theory. Indeed, how can one resist the temptation to apply a psychoanalytically inspired investigation to Freud himself when interpreting the abundant material brought to light by his biographers?"[9]

Unfortunately many authors fall under the spell of this temptation, whether mystifying Freud's work, reducing it to a product of Jewish culture, or "psychoanalyzing" Judaism.

Freud pointed out that all attempts at psychoanalyzing cultures were no more than exercises in analogical thinking. An analogy, people seem to forget, doesn't correspond to the thing itself. There is something humorous about the certainty with which these authors claim to be right in their final understanding of the key to psychoanalysis, especially since they express opposite certainties.

David Bakan's *Sigmund Freud and the Jewish Mystical Tradition*, for instance, wants to illustrate in detail the similarities between psychoanalysis and esoteric Jewish mysticism. Even though he acknowledges that it is impossible to demonstrate that Freud had any deep knowledge of the doctrine and method of the Kabbala, Bakan chooses to ignore his own awareness of the fact and speaks of a "Kabbalistic spirit" that supposedly aroused strong mystical feelings in the founder of psychoanalysis.[10] The author

---

[9] Le Rider, *Modernité viennoise*, p. 13.
[10] Bakan, *Sigmund Freud and the Jewish Mystical Tradition*, pp. 305-19.

presents no evidence that might lend any plausibility to the idea that Jewish mysticism was somehow transmitted to a Jew who not only had no direct or indirect knowledge of the Kabbala but also stated unambiguously throughout his life that he was not a believer. In addition, what Freud said he most admired in Judaism was precisely its lack of mystical elements. This is not to say that Freud was totally ignorant of the existence of the Kabbala, or that he in any way denied the links between the Kabbala and Jewish tradition. According to Yerushalmi, Freud owed much to the rationalist tendency in nineteenth-century philosophy that recognized the breadth and the tradition of Jewish mysticism, although it saw the Kabbala as an inauthentic form of the Mosaic doctrine.[11]

In *Sigmund, fils de Jacob*, Marianne Krüll attempts a psychoanalytic investigation of Freud's life. Krüll endeavors to discuss the links between psychoanalysis and Judaism on the basis of Freud's relationship with his father. The book's central thesis is that Jakob Freud's estrangement from traditional Judaism generated in him intense feelings of guilt that eventually affected his son. Krüll tries to analyze the relationship between father and son in terms of what she takes to be an interplay of feelings of guilt and narcissistic identifications, and concludes that psychoanalysis is the product of psychological motifs related to Freud's conflicts with his father. Why should we consider Krüll's study to be a psychoanalytic work? If she uses Freudian concepts as mere categories to be applied to biography, one must conclude that her work is no more that a speculative reading with psychoanalytic pretensions. This kind of exercise tells us more about the author than its subject.

Freud analyzed his own dreams and parapraxes in order to illustrate his theories and their functioning; he never had the intention of "revealing" their origins. Yet he suspected that he would become the object of some sort of biographical speculation. In this regard, he invoked the words with which Shakespeare's Caliban answers Prospero: "You taught me language; and my profit on't is, I know how to curse."[12]

Estelle Roith's effort to discuss Freud's theory of feminine sexuality is a superfluous exegesis of Freud's work, based upon what the author calls his "unwillingness to confront the issues surrounding his relationship with his *mother*."[13] She claims with minimal evidence that Freud's concepts

---

[11] Yerushalmi, *Freud's Moses*, pp. 124-25, n. 16.
[12] Quoted in Jones, *The Life and Works of Sigmund Freud*, vol. 3, p. 145.
[13] Roith, *The Riddle of Freud: Jewish Influences on his Theory of Female Sexuality*, p. 4.

of femininity are heavily influenced by the place reserved for women in Jewish culture. How can one say anything about psychoanalytic theory on the basis of interpretations of Freud's relationship with his mother, father, or any other person except his patients? It was only by listening to his patients that Freud discovered the formations of the unconscious and their structure. And by no means were all of Freud's female patients Jewish.

Roith emphasizes repressive aspects of Judaism in order to support the idea that Judaism is a patriarchal doctrine that discriminates against women. Her totalizing interpretation ignores the significance of sex and women in the Talmud.[14] Furthermore, she disregards the transformations that Freud's theory of feminine sexuality undergoes throughout his work.

In his *Freud lecteur de la Bible*, Théo Pfrimmer advances the thesis that psychoanalysis is a legitimate product of the Biblical universe. He argues that the Bible exerted a powerful influence on the discovery of psychoanalysis. To support his hypothesis, the author points to about 400 Biblical quotations gleaned from Freud's written works, his correspondence and his *obiter dicta*. Pfrimmer's conclusions reduce psychoanalysis to Freud's imaginary identifications with Biblical characters. Pfrimmer goes so far as to suggest that psychoanalysis has a theological sources, which not only contradicts what is known about Freud's views on religion but also clashes with his explicit declarations of atheism.

In *D'Œdipe à Moïse: Freud et la conscience juive*, Marthe Robert argues that Freud's psychological drama, springing from ambivalent feelings about his father, contributed to the elaboration of his discovery. She argues that *Der Mann Moses und die monotheistische Religion* is influenced by such feelings and shows Freud's desire to become the "son" of his own works.[15]

---

[14] The feminine is one of the six important themes of the Mishna (the collection of oral laws that form the basic part of the Talmud). Concerning the analysis of the body and sexuality in rabbinical Judaism, Daniel Boyarin – starting from the assumption that the Patristic Church saw Judaism as a "carnal" religion, as opposed to Catholicism – argues that rabbinical Judaism was based on a number of views of the human body that were different from those held by Christianity. To rabbinical Jews, the human being is defined as a body animated by a soul. It is the soul that gives life to the body, the existence of which defines what is human. See Boyarin, *Carnal Israel*, passim.

[15] Reducing the discovery of psychoanalysis to an Oedipal conflict and to its creator's imaginary identifications is reductive and erroneous. Nonetheless, Robert provides an excellent overview to Freud's contribution to his culture in a society that viewed difference with hostility. She distinguishes bewteen his Jewish culture of origin and his culture of reference. Culture of origin includes all that conditions emotional attitudes, the earliest identifications and the perceptions of childhood. Culture of reference implies reflection.

In his *A Godless Jew*, Peter Gay's juxtaposition of the concepts of Jew and atheist, and his definition of the former only in religious terms go no further than to demonstrate Freud's atheism, laying too much emphasis on evidence of Freud's nonreligious upbringing. Convinced that Judaism was not handed down to Freud, Gay makes no mention of the symbolic link that Freud maintained with it. On the other hand, his thesis that Freud identified with Moses in his analysis of *Der Mann Moses und die monotheistische Religion* is in no way different from the would-be psychological fabrications that so many authors, whether psychoanalysts or historians, indulge in when they write about Freud. He remarks: "Freud made Moses an Egyptian so that he, Freud, could be the first true Moses to his people."[16]

This statement, as with many others, proves once again the spell cast by Freud's ideas. In discussing Freud, everyone wants to play the psychoanalyst! Applying psychoanalytic concepts to Freud the man and to Jewish culture inevitably leads to a quagmire: the use of psychoanalysis as a tool for reading the very origin of psychoanalysis amounts to reductionism and misses altogether the understanding of Freud's Jewishness as an ongoing construction.

Psychoanalysis Between Reason and Myth

Mezan's propositions concerning the resonance of Judaism in psychoanalysis follow a different path. He makes no attempt to psychoanalyze Freud or to use psychoanalytic tools to demonstrate that Judaism is an ancestor of psychoanalysis. For this very reason, his criticisms directed at those who tend to confuse Freud's discovery with Freud's culture of origin are cogent and pertinent. However, Mezan presents the reader with only one Freud – the Freud who questions religion in *The Future of an Illusion*. There is no hint of the Freud who searches for historical truth – understood as a truth that transcends the materiality of facts – in myths, fables, works of fiction and religion, and accounts for an order of thought different from that of reason and consciousness. With regard to Judaism, Mezan is also partial: he discusses only its religious dimension.

Freud was most certainly an atheist. His curious correspondence with the Protestant minister Oskar Pfister, in which he discusses at length the relationship between psychoanalytic and religious discourses, shows

---

[16] Gay, *A Godless Jew*, p. 150.

that he was always careful to distance his discipline from a discursive field ruled by a belief in a single truth. The same emphasis on the incompleteness of knowledge is evident in the "Two Encyclopaedia Articles" written by Freud. Psychoanalysis cannot be structured like a philosophical system founded on the logic of consciousness, which seeks "to grasp the whole universe with the help of these [sharply defined basic concepts] and, once it is completed, [has] no room for fresh discoveries or better understanding." It must remain constrained by its own experience, "always incomplete and always ready to correct or modify its theories." At the end of these considerations, Freud raises the question of how close psychoanalysis is to the field of science, comparing his discipline to physics or chemistry – sciences that in their theoretical corpus contain concepts that are important although they "lack clarity." Their "postulates are provisional" and they will find more precise definitions in future works.[17] This is consistent with his words to Pfister about making analysts "*lay* curers of souls"[18] and his hope that, by baptizing psychoanalysis in the cult of the god Logos, he will protect it from the danger of turning into just another of the religious discourses of modernity.[19]

If one takes into consideration the difference between the actual development of science and its reception by a culture, it is possible to find in Freud's thoughts a definition of science as a discovery derived from an experience of confrontation with otherness. Psychoanalysis as such meets this fundamental prerequisite: Freud once observed that analytic practice – the art of interpreting the patient's free associations – introduced "a fresh scale of values in scientific thought"[20] and created an absolutely original model of scientificity. Such a model relates to the act of speech, to what is said and to the unsayable that expresses itself through the formations of the unconscious (symptoms, dreams, parapraxes, silences, interruptions, etc.). Freud's invention unveils an-Other scene: the scene of a thought that obeys criteria different from those of rational, conscious thinking. Against the grain of *Aufklärung* rationality, which privileges coherence and identity as forms of truth, psychoanalysis presents itself as a method of listening to

---

[17] *SE*, vol. 18, pp. 253-54 ["Two Encyclopaedia Articles"]

[18] Letter of Nov. 25, 1928, *Freud/Pfister, Psychoanalysis and Faith*.

[19] See *SE*, vol. 21, p. 68. [*The Future of an Illusion*]. Logos means not just "reason," as is commonly thought, but also the discursive speech of Greek orators in the assembly of the polis, the locus of the city's social regulation (See Chapter 3 of Vernant, *Myth and Thought among the Greeks*).

[20] *SE*, vol. 20, p. 43. [*An Autobiographical Study*]

the unconscious, the nonidentical, the deformed, always obeying the logic of the Other.

Nineteenth-century psychology, which presented itself as a science, considered madness, as well as sensory phenomena, perceptions, images, beliefs and so on, as mere mistakes of meaning or purely illusory realities. Going in the opposite direction, Freud began his practice by listening to all of these marginal phenomena, drawing from them the elements of a new and original scientific theory and allowing the emergence of new possibilities of thinking and speech. He adhered to a position that would not yield to any previous knowledge or system of thought.

Akin to the language of dreams, as well as to the expressions of primitive languages, Freud paid attention to ideas that do not necessarily respond to Aristotelian logic but may include the coincidence of opposites. He paid attention to the different logic expressed by the structure of primary processes and psychic causality, for which a new understanding and a new vocabulary needed to be invented.

"Under the guise of a dignified gray, beige and pink stucco façade and a new slate roof, this is how all the psychoanalytic houses of the Freudian Diaspora are built. The foundations are on the one hand tragic-mythical and, on the other, Biblical and Evangelical; the walls are sometimes made of scientistic brick, sometimes built with the stones of Gnostic agnosticism, the whole structure being cemented with substandard linguistic mortar."[21] In this way Serge Leclaire underscored the strange architecture of a new practice that, by breaking with the same, introduced us to the land of the Other.

Freud used the theoretical frame of reference of the positivist science of his time. He referred to medicine, neurology, biology, anthropology, and evolutionism. But he also carefully listened to the speech of his patients and to the cultural domains they opened to him. A veritable weaver, he wove together threads from Greek mythology, Jewish ethics, Eastern and Western philosophy, literature, drama, and poetry.

He was ahead of the most advanced studies on myths: he understood the function of myths as symbolic narratives, mostly produced in a remote past and transmitted in present-day reality, constructed to convey *a truth about origins*. Myths – tales that authorize customs, rituals, and beliefs, or sanction changes in them[22] – are situated between mastery and knowledge

---

[21] Serge Leclaire, *Le Pays de l'Autre*, p. 30.
[22] For an in-depth study of the function of myth in culture, see Eliade, *Myth and Reality*.

of nature, and this endows them with symbolic efficacy. Freud advised analysts to make use of the history of civilizations and mythology. As his correspondence with Fliess illustrates, from the inception of psychoanalysis Freud identified the analogies and the relations existing between fantasy and myth, and studied them as imaginary and symbolic constructions that allow human beings to provide possible answers to the unknown.

Recognizing their historical, social, and individual function, psychoanalysis gives to mythical constructions their appropriate value, inscribing them within the discourse of scientific reason. As Freud wrote to Einstein: "It may perhaps seem to you as though our theories are a kind of mythology and, in the present case, not even an agreeable one. But does not every science come in the end to a kind of mythology like this? Cannot the same be said to-day of your own Physics?"[23]

What Is the Significance of Judaism to Psychoanalysis?

How can we read Freud so as to acquire a better understanding of *the influence of Freud's experience of his own Jewishness on the formulation of the psychoanalytic method and clinical practice?* And how might this be done without writing a psycho-biography of Freud, by psychoanalyzing Judaism, or by Judaizing psychoanalysis?

In his study of Freud's writing, Solal Rabinovitch recommends that we read Freud with Freud: "just as he is in the writing of his own theoretical search."[24] Reading Freud with Freud disallows any reading of the events in his life and in the construction of psychoanalysis solely in terms of the difference between latent content and manifest content, which re-

---

The prologue to Graves and Pataj's *Hebrew Myths: The Book of Genesis* includes an interesting discussion of the applicability of the Greek notion of mythology to Biblical narrative. Lydia Flem, in *Freud the Man*, emphasizes the importance of Greek thought and myth in psychoanalysis. She observes that there are clear marks left by the Greek myths in Freud's science of dreams. Oedipus and Narcissus, two major treasuries of Greek mythology, were adopted by psychoanalysis as privileged conceptual figures for the foundation of the unconscious and the formation of the ego.

[23] *SE*, vol. 22, pp. 211. ["Why War?"] Freud called his theory of the drive "our mythology." The drive lies *between* the psychological and the somatic, *between* what has received meaning and what has not been inscribed. It is the myth of the Diaspora of the Freudian subject, what lies *in between* body and language.

[24] Rabinovitch, "Écriture et défiguration, une lecture du *Moïse* de Freud." *Rue Decartes* 8/9 (1993)

duces psychoanalysis to the imaginary identifications of its creator. Only a literal reading of Freud's writings – reading Freud's letter step by step, underlining the gaps in his text – will transcend the level of opinion and psychologizing.

One reading that has the merit of not "applying" psychoanalysis to Freud himself, nor Judaism to psychoanalysis, is that of Yerushalmi in *Freud's Moses: Judaism Terminable and Interminable*. A historian of Judaism, Yerushalmi attempts to analyze the "Jewish question" that permeates psychoanalysis, as well as to find out the truth about Freud's own Jewishness, resorting solely to his writings and letters, always questioning just how Freud practiced his Jewishness beyond the obvious religious signifiers. The entire book is dedicated to an analysis of *Der Mann Moses und die monotheistische Religion*, in which Freud points to a new concept of truth that Western historiography and science find difficult to deal with and that, according to Yerushalmi, is implied by Judaism in its very foundations – not as a concept, to be sure, but as a way of grasping the past not only as something that "subjugates," but also "nourishes."[25] Jakob Freud's dedication in the family Bible he gave to his son Sigmund upon his thirty-fifth birthday is another strand in Yerushalmi's analysis. As a historian, he suggests that the way psychoanalysis relates to the history of the analysand is quite similar to the way Jews obey the exhortation to *zakhor* (remember), the obligation to remember the history of the people of Abraham, Isaac, and Jacob. Since Biblical times this commandment has had the function – as will be shown in greater detail in Chapter 5 – of reaffirming, with each remembrance, the founding act of the Covenant.

The parallel between Judaism and psychoanalysis drawn by Yerushalmi, endows Freud's text with new life. And – in contrast with others who, like Gay, believe Freud's Jewishness had little or no influence on his thought – he shows that, quite apart from Freud's Spinozan non-belief in the Jewish religion, he was faithful to his Jewishness. What does "science" mean, and what does "Jewish" mean? These are the two questions that Yerushalmi raises in his book, without, however, quite answering them. In this way, as Jacques Derrida has observed, Freud leaves to the future not only the task of redefining the concept of science and of the category "Jew" but also the question of the relations between psychoanalysis and Judaism.[26] Is it possible to say, on the strength of Yerushalmi's

---

[25] Yerushalmi, *Freud's Moses*, p. 78.
[26] Derrida, *Archive Fever*, p. 52.

reading, that the riddle of the connection between psychoanalysis and Judaism is at the limit of the "navel of the dream," which belongs to the order of "non-interpretation," or of the urgency of producing new meanings? Isn't this his intention when, at the end of his study of *Moses*, he presents a "Monologue with Freud," resorting to the strategy of sending a letter to a dead man, who cannot reply?

Derrida discusses Yerushalmi's work in depth in his *Archive Fever*. First it is necessary to locate the philosopher's attempt to read Judaism as writing. The "Hebrew" discomforts of repetition, exile, wandering, and nomadism are, to Derrida, the very movement of the meaning of writing, which exists only in a network of past and future elements, in an economy of traces. In "Edmond Jabès and the Question of the Book" Derrida conceives the autonomy of writing in Jabès's poems as the paradigm of "a certain Judaism as the birth and passion of writing. The passion *of* writing, the love and endurance of the letter whose subject is not decidably the Jew or the Letter itself." And it is in the wake of this passion that in the same essay he invokes the letter as "the common root of a people and of writing."[27] And what could "the love and endurance of the letter itself" possibly mean but that the act of reading is an encounter with Otherness?

In "Freud and the Scene of Writing" Derrida uses psychoanalysis to discuss how the symbolic arises, how the non-symbolic leads to the symbolic. In the Freudian model of machines and apparatuses, the unconscious is a writing that weaves itself with differences and trajectories, and sends or delegates representatives and deputies that can only be understood a posteriori. Writing is the possibility of instituting. According to Derrida repetition is present from the beginning, but it is never repetition of the same.

In *Archive Fever* Derrida discusses the relations between differential repetition and the concept of archive – which should be distinguished from the notion of experience of memory, from the idea of return to the origin and the meaning of the archaic. The concept of archive has to do with something that lies beyond the resurrection of the event: it includes in its memory the Greek word *arkhé*, meaning both "beginning" and "command." *Arkhé* "coordinates two principles in one: the principle according to nature or history, *there* where things *commence* – physical, historical, or ontological principle – but also the principle according to the law... *there* where authority, social order are exercised, *in this place* from which *order* is given – nomological principle."[28]

---

[27] Derrida, *Writing and Difference*, p. 64.
[28] Derrida, *Archive Fever*, p. 1.

It is clear that the issue of psychoanalytic temporality has steered Derrida's attention in this book toward Judaism. He asks what the archive turns into when it is inscribed in the body itself, as in circumcision, and he himself replies that in each act of circumcision there is nothing that causes a return to the origin, but rather the beginning of a new Jew. Circumcision introduces the individual into the collective order, but preserves his relationship with the real, what is not identifiable and, as such, becomes a trace. Circumcision as an archive is expectation for the future, the experience of an identity that can be declared and announced only on the basis of what is to come in the future.

The date of Sigmund Freud's circumcision was registered in the family Bible next to the dedication that his father wrote to him when he gave the book to his son for his birthday. Three documents in the Freud Archives (the circumcision, the registration of the circumcision, and the dedication); a double inscription (one in the body, the other in the symbolic): these are the marks of Freud's Jewish cultural experience in the book that is the Book.

About Freud's relation with the Book of Books, his own testimony is eloquent: "My deep engrossment in the Bible story (almost as soon as I had learnt the art of reading) had, as I recognized much later, an enduring effect upon the direction of my interest."[29] This acknowledgment is part of Freud's brief outline, in his "autobiographical study," of his intellectual formation, showing the influence of the Bible and the importance of the Jewish ethos in his upbringing. Led by a sort of curiosity that was directed more at human relationships than at nature, Freud says that from an early age what most interested him was the Bible, the study of the law, and social activities. The works of three thinkers, he says, were fundamental to his choices: Darwin's theories; the writings of Goethe, which led him to study medicine; and the work of Ernst Brücke, the master who influenced him the most by teaching him the value of scientific observation.

Jakob Freud was the first to call attention to the precocious and profound impression that the polysemy of the Book of Books had on his son's spirit. The loving and delicate dedication he wrote for him in the family Bible is the most truthful and sincere testimony we have about the origins of Freud's relationship with knowledge. After he had re-bound the yellowed and torn pages he had used to teach his son his first lessons in Bible reading, Jakob wrote his dedication, all of it in Hebrew, in *melitzah* –

---

[29] *SE*, vol. 20, p. 8. [*An Autobiographical Study*]

a process whereby the old Talmudists put together a new text assembling fragments or expressions taken from the Bible or other sacred books. In fact, the gift and the dedication were an expression of the old father's pride and joy on the birthday of his son, who – so he believed – had more intelligence in his little toe then he himself had in his entire brain. Here is the dedication:

> Son who is dear to me, Shelomoh. In the seventh in the days of the years of your life the Spirit of the Lord began to move you and spoke within you: Go, read in my Book that I have written and there will burst open for you the wellsprings of understanding, knowledge, and wisdom. Behold, it is the Book of Books, from which sages have excavated and lawmakers learned knowledge and justice. A vision of the Almighty did you see; you heard and strove to do, and you soared upon the wings of the Spirit.
>
> Since then the book has been stored like the fragments of the tablets in an ark with me. For the day on which your years were filled to five and thirty I have put upon it a cover of new skin and have called it: "Spring up, O well, sing ye unto it!" And I have presented it to you as a memorial and as a reminder of love from your father, who loves you with everlasting love.
>
> Jakob Son of R. She[lomoh] Freid *[sic]*
> In the capital city Vienna 29 Nisan [5]651 6 May [1]891[30]

Jakob's subtle lesson is clear: this old Jew from Galicia who had been given an orthodox rabbinical upbringing, but who had also been affected by the Enlightenment, saw the Scriptures as more than a collection of narratives from which a dogmatic sort of knowledge may be extracted: "Spring up, O well, sing ye unto it!" To him, the Book was an accumulation of letters that preserved an inexhaustible store of knowledge, an infinite possibility of associations. It is just as important to underscore the father's tactful gesture toward his scientist son: by using the particular form of the *melitzah* in his dedication, Jakob suggests that Freud's absorption of his readings of the Book as a child had a decisive impact on the way he grasped, affectively and intellectually, the urgent issues of his day.

If for Jakob the Scriptures were an inexhaustible source of food to quench the hunger for knowledge, to the "adventurer"[31] sailing the turbu-

---

[30] Jakob Freud's comment on his son's intelligence and the dedication are quoted in Yerushalmi's *Freud's Moses*, pp. 63 and 71 respectively. To Yerushalmi, the composition of the dedication demonstrates that Freud's father mastered the Bible (at least the prophetic texts used in the liturgy) and expresses the mentality of a traditional Jew, whatever his degree of religiosity.

[31] Freud saw himself as an adventurer; as he wrote Fliess on Feb. 1, 1900, "I am by tem-

lent seas of the unconscious, psychoanalysis ought to search, in this inexhaustible source of the real, for a guarantee of its existence and efficacy.

Judaism sees the Torah as an inexhaustible source of learning and wisdom, in which one relies most of all on textuality,[32] so that meanings multiply. The reader of the sacred narratives of Jewish culture is instructed to navigate the river of polysemy, to deconstruct the text, to scatter his interest far and wide and to introduce issues that are never complete in themselves. This age-old practice of reading the Scriptures in Jewish culture is what gives support to Lévinas's claim that Judaism is permanently fated to remain incomplete and to feed on its own insatiable hunger. To him, the Talmudic reading of the Biblical Text emerges from the encounter with the Foreign, which implies ensuring the relationship between the reader and Infinity. And the idea of Infinity, to Lévinas, assumes the "separation of the same with regard to the other," not as pure opposition between the two terms, but "as non-integrateable."[33]

Lévinas found a balance between Western and Jewish philosophy remaining faithful both to the conceptual discourse of the Greeks and to Hebrew tradition. In the latter, he claims to have found elements to support his conviction that ethics is not a field of knowledge among others, but the primary philosophy[34]: the philosophy of the relationship with the Other. Ethics, seen as a form of transcendence, is properly understood as the secularization of the sacred. If morality involves the repression of desire, ethics arises from the rediscovery of the Other and translates the "condition of the atheist," the paradigm of the *separated being*.

Lévinas's philosophy resists the simplifications and criticisms that attempt to characterize it as a religion-tinged thought. Quite to the contrary, he believes that atheism has to do with the thinking concerned with alterity – that is, the thinking that avoids resorting either to rationalization or to the Sacred itself as privileged places of meaning. His concern with otherness provided him with the starting point for the development of the idea that it is possible to invert Western philosophy's concept of a God that is not to be identified with Being. In this way Lévinas is able to es-

---

perament nothing but a conquistador – an adventurer, if you want it translated – with all the curiosity, daring, and tenacity of a man of this sort." Freud, *Complete Letters of Sigmund Freud to Wilhelm Fliess, 1887-1904*, trans. and ed. by Jeffrey Moussaieff Masson.

[32] "Textuality" is used here to refer to the potency of the letter as generator of meaning. This theme, together with the intertextuality of the Sacred Text, will be further elaborated in Chapter 5, below.

[33] Lévinas, *Totality and Infinity*, p. 53.

[34] Lévinas, *Ethique et infini*, p. 91.

tablish vital links between the Talmudic universe and modern thought.

By raising once again the question of Being through ethics, Lévinas was also able to cull from a kind of hegemonic and univocal Judaism a different Judaism, one that asserts itself through difference and sees itself as unfinished. Lévinas's ideas are an original contribution to the question of the Other. The Other "is other with respect to a term whose essence is to remain at the point of departure, to serve as *entry* into the relation, to be the same not relatively but absolutely."[35] Against the sterile ontology of the identity of the Same, Lévinas attempts to transmit to contemporary philosophers *the appeal to the other*, the only possible resistance against any hegemonic and egalitarian ideal.[36]

The passion for the foreign, for what cannot be assimilated, is as clear in Freud's works as in Lévinas's: the writings of both authors are marked by an exteriority rooted in the immediacy of an opening to the known-unknown, the *unheimlich*, to use Freud's preferred term, or, to quote Lévinas, "the Stranger who disturbs the being at home with oneself [*le chez soi*]."[37] If in Freud's strategies for the creation and assertion of psychoanalysis he clearly demanded a separation and distancing from the compact majority, an option which throughout his life and work is expressed by a *desire for difference*, in Lévinas's thought what is particularly evident is the movement away from the identical, or rather the desire for an *untiring struggle for the Other*.

It is well known that psychoanalytic issues, especially interpretation, prompted Lacan to take an interest in Judaism. In *L'Éthique de la psychanalyse* Lacan made precise observations about the origins of modern

---

[35] Lévinas, *Totality and Infinity*, p. 36.

[36] Lévinas's thought is particularly important for the present work not only because of its contribution to a richer reading of Judaism, but also for its possible relations with psychoanalysis. Such a conjunction, which has been commented on by some authors, is quite illuminating, and is one of the guidelines of this book. The notion of Other that Lacan introduces to psychoanalysis is quite close to Lévinas. "It was through Lévinas that the Other entered ethics, and through Lacan that the Other was affirmed in psychoanalysis." Assoun, *op. cit.*, p. 12. The texts by Monique Schneider ("A proximidade de Lévinas e o *Nebenmensch* freudiano") and Luiz Cláudio Figueiredo ("O interesse de Lévinas para a psicanálise: desinteresse do rosto") also testify to the importance of Lévinas's thought for psychoanalysis. Through Lévinas's notion of proximity, Schneider offers an insightful and original reading of Freud's notion of the *Nebenmensch*, or fellow-man, as it was originally formulated in the 1895 *Entwurf*. Figueiredo reads Lévinas for a more comprehensive view of psychoanalytic temporality. *Caderno de Subjetividade*, Pontifícia Universidade Católica de São Paulo, São Paulo, 1997.

[37] Lévinas, *Totality and Infinity*, p. 39.

science: "modern science, the kind that was born with Galileo, could only have developed out of Biblical or Judaic ideology, and not out of ancient philosophy or the Aristotelian tradition."[38] Jean-Claude Milner observes: "Here lies the difference between Kojève and Lacan: the former attributes to Christianity, particularly to the dogma of Incarnation... a decisive role in the emergence of science: now, this dogma is precisely what separates Christianity from Judaism; Lacan attributes a decisive role to Judaism and what is left of Judaism in Christianity – that is, precisely the letter."[39]

If it is possible to agree with Milner on Lacan's emphasis on the function of the letter – what cannot be fixed or contained in a signification or image – in the development of science, one understands all the better the relationship that he also establishes between Jewish reading and psychoanalytic interpretation. In both, according to Lacan, the effect of the persistence of the letter is a practice of reading that allows the subject to say something that comes from a place other than that of rational thinking.

Lacan stresses that the analyst should be able to carry the art of reading the letters and the text to its utmost consequences. The analyst should look to the ethical order that supports what lies beyond the merely exegetic intentions of reading: "the Jew... is the one who knows how to read, that is: from the letter, he keeps distance from its word, and in it finds the interval, until he makes an interpretation there."[40]

Evoking this association between the Jewish signifier and "he who knows how to read," Jean-Pierre Winter demonstrates how such a relation makes explicit the atheist's position. Here a paradox should be pointed out: Judaism requires that its interpreter, the Talmudist, assume the position of an atheist, one who will not block the advent of the word, making a new "golden calf" out of the Text. The atheistic basis in Jewish thought, the history of Jewish monotheism allow a nonbeliever like Freud

---

[38] Lacan, *The Ethics of Psychoanalysis*, p. 122.

[39] Jean-Claude Milner, *L'Œuvre claire*, p. 71. For a full grasp of Lacan's proposition, it is of fundamental importance to understand the distinction between the three registers discussed in his theory: *the real, the symbolic* and *the imaginary*. The real is what escapes all symbolization and is always a remainder, what cannot be symbolized because it resists absolute characterization. The symbolic is the sum total of signifiers, marked by the absence of a signifier that might totalize them. The imaginary is the system of crystallized significations or meanings. In the sense of a character, the letter is, in Lacanian theory, both the material support of the signifier and what is distinguished from it due to the fact that it can signal the intrusion of the radically other. See the entry *lettre* in *Dictionnaire de la Psychanalyse*, ed. by Roland Chemama and Bernard Vandermersch , pp. 172-175.

[40] Lacan, "Radiophonie," *Scilicet* 2-3, 1970, p. 80; also see "Proposition," *Scilicet*, 1968, p. 21.

to feel he belongs to the Jewish people without being religious.[41] This point of view differs from Gay's or Mezan's, authors who see in Freud's atheism nothing more than the effects of the Enlightenment: in his relationship with the text and with thought, Freud's atheism is systematically Jewish.

---

[41] Winter, "Transmission et Talmude," in *Bulletin interne de l'EFP*, vol. II, June 1979.

Chapter 3
Exile and Foreignness

> *If we have not been strangers elsewhere, we must discover our Egypt. Our symbolic "foreignness."*
>
> PAUL RICŒUR[1]

When he asked himself or was asked about his Jewish identity, Freud's answer never settled on an easy definition. Although he considered himself a Jew for willingly facing an unending struggle with the "homogenized" and "compact majority,"[2] whether within or outside of Judaism, he paradoxically declared it impossible to define such an identity – not least out of his strong sense that all identities are deceptive. One might say Freud invented an absolutely unique way to practice and demonstrate the kind of Jew he was, unclassifiable in terms of what, in his time and ours, is known as Judaism. This fundamentally positive trait in the construction of his own Jewishness directly affected the invention of psychoanalysis, both through the social exclusion of its inventor – which, according to Freud himself, helped him face the resistance against psychoanalysis – and through what I want to call his "becoming-Jew."

Becoming, as the term is used by Deleuze and Guattari, refers to a process seen as a reality in its own right rather than as merely the transformation of one thing into another. It implies breaking with existing models, so that the subject is forced into unknown paths, if he or she is willing to follow them. It is a process with real existence, since it is neither an imaginary imitation nor a symbolic analogy, but is connected to a single, unique expressivity. For instance, *becoming-woman* implies the impossibility of a final being, for there is no woman into which the subject is transformed, not even when one is a woman. Similarly, "becoming-Jew" implies the impossibility of being a Jew, for what *is* is becoming – an action that encourages the subject to challenge any sense of the identical and to reinvent oneself as an Other.

---

[1] Interview with Jean Daniel in *Les grandes questions de la Philo*, ed. by Marie-Reine Monville. Paris: Maisonneuve et Larose, 1998.

[2] *SE*, vol. 20, pp 273-74. [Address to the Society of B'nai B'rith]

In the preface to the Hebrew edition of *Totem and Taboo*, after stating that he neither professes the religion of his parents nor believes in any Jewish nationalist ideal, but also declaring that he in no way denies being a member of the Jewish people, Freud asks his imaginary interlocutor a question, the answer to which suggests the impossibility of defining an identity, a Jewish "essential nature." "If the question were put to him: 'Since you have abandoned all these common characteristics of your countrymen, what is there left to you that is Jewish?' he would reply: 'A very great deal, and probably its very essence.' He could not now express that essence clearly in words; but someday, no doubt, it will become accessible to the scientific mind."[3] It was precisely this "essence" that remained in him, as he confided to his colleagues: "plenty of other things remained over to make the attraction of Jewry and Jews irresistible – many obscure emotional forces, which were the more powerful the less they could be expressed in words."[4]

Although Freud can precisely spell out his difference with Judaism, he has no words to express a mark that questions him. One of his most categorical statements on his limit-experience with the "known-unknown" is to be found in a letter he sent to Barbara Low on the death of his friend and colleague David Edler: "I can easily imagine how he, too, must have suffered under the bitterness of these times. We were both Jews and knew of each other that we carried that miraculous thing in common, which – inaccessible to any analysis so far – makes the Jew."[5] This is a curious statement, which obeys the logic of an invisible and ineffable presence manifested to the subject. It is as though there were in Freud something beyond Jewish identity, an unrepresentable and unnamable Jewishness that expressed itself as the constant search for an Other in himself. Put differently, the expression of Freud's Jewishness was his permanent exodus from a fixed, unchanging identity, that might be mirrored in some religious or political mimesis.

In so constructing his Jewishness, Freud constantly struggled against the coercive force of the ties and models that generate intolerance in any community: religion expressed as idolatry, that is, taking away one's freedom to reinvent oneself ceaselessly once one has chosen to be a Jew. Freud saw this freezing of movement as one of the detrimental effects of

---

[3] *SE*, vol. 13, p. xv. [*Totem and Taboo*, Preface to the Hebrew Translation.]

[4] *SE*, vol. 20, pp. 273-74. [Address to the Society of B'nai B'rith]

[5] Letter of Apr. 19, 1936, *Letters of Sigmund Freud*.

religious dogmatism.⁶ If, then, his admirable reflection on the enigma of his Jewish condition allowed him to recognize himself as a Jew "who has yet never repudiated his people,"⁷ on the other hand religiosity, fundamentalism, and everything that prevents the subject from relating to the unknown, was to be rejected. Freud made it quite clear that although he acknowledged belonging to his people of origin, this was no reason to deny that Judaism, for all its spiritual progress, was threatened by fundamentalism. Precisely this insistence on something beyond religion allows Freud to describe himself as an atheist, an agnostic, and a Jew. This same insistence allows Isaac Bashevis Singer to express through one of his characters: "I can deny God, but I cannot stop being a Jew – contradictory and strange as these words may sound."⁸ In the autonomy of the subject vis-à-vis the heteronomy of the law, Jewishness may transcend religion. Whereas dogmatic religious belief merely encourages the subject's resistance to the individual appropriation of the signifiers of a history that must be constantly remade and invented so that the new may arise.

If Freud's critique of Judaism may be taken as a sign of his deep-rooted unfaithfulness to the religion of his parents, it should be borne in mind that he nonetheless expressed an equally deep-rooted adherence to Jewish ethics as an age-old practice of alterity. Freud is close to those who practice and conceive of Judaism as an ethics, a relation to life and the unexpected. In this sense he created conditions under which he could constantly enter and exit from the Jewish community, in a process that had a point of departure but no points of closure.

For Derrida Jewishness is the expression of a "coming-to-be," but with the following qualification: "the Jew's identification with himself does not exist. 'Jew' would be the other name of this impossibility of being himself."⁹ The writings and poetry of Edmond Jabès likewise describe the

---

⁶ In an emotional letter to his fiancée Martha Bernays, on the occasion of the suicide of his friend and colleague Nathan Weiss, the son of an eminent doctor of rabbinical law, Freud describes the mortification he experienced during the funeral –which a number of Christians attended – when the rabbi made a savage and cruel speech marked by fanaticism and intolerance. Letter of Sept. 16, 1883, *Letters of Sigmund Freud*, pp. 58-66.

⁷ *SE*, vol. 13, p. xv. [*Totem and Taboo*, Preface to the Hebrew Translation]

⁸ Singer, *The Manor and the Estate*, p. 428.

⁹ Derrida, *Writing and Difference*, p. 112. [*Translator's Note*: The last sentence in this quotation does not appear in the English edition; it was translated directly from the French text, which reads: "Mais l'identité à soi du Juif, n'existe peut-être pas. Juif serait l'autre nom de cette impossibilité d'etre soi."]

process of becoming-Jew. In "Judaïsme et écriture" the poet asks rhetorically: "What authorizes me to consider myself a Jew?"[10] This question provides the very basis for the practice of a certain kind of Judaism achieved through writing, in which the writing of oneself as a Jew is a self-nullifying act by dint of its very representation. Lévinas also explicitly states that what marks him as a Jew is the impossibility of always seeing himself as "the same."[11] The Brazilian psychoanalyst Chaim Katz similarly writes: "Judaism is characterized by unfinishedness."[12] This becoming-Jew within Judaism itself, which is the affirmation of a unique Jewishness rather than a reference to any collective identity, may be associated, from a Deleuzian-Guattarian perspective, with the becoming-woman of a woman.[13]

Psychoanalysis creates conditions in which subjects may come to experience what is foreign to them; Freud's invention brings about a radical separation between the subject and the identical, which finally leads the subject to experience what Juan-David Nasio names "exile." "I would not hesitate to state that psychoanalysis should tend to create a radical separation, an essential loss that reorganizes the subject's psychological reality, a loss I call exile."[14] This exile consists in making the subject seek – in the discomfort of repetition and in the gradual deconstruction of one's own idolatry (narcissism of the ego and imperatives of the superego) – what is most foreign to one: the confrontation with the unknown. To experience analytic exile is a learning of alterity: it allows the subject to search for a word to name what is both intimate and foreign.

The clinical tool of free association, the fundamental rule of psychoanalytic work, shows how the act of speech breaks with the identical. To speak is, as Maurice Blanchot puts it, "to seek the source of meaning in the prefix that the words *exile, exodus, existence, exteriority* and *estrangement* are committed to unfolding in the various modes of experience; a prefix that for us designates distance and separation as the origin of all 'positive value.'"[15]

---

[10] Jabès, "Judaïsme et écriture," in M. Moscovici and J.M. Rey (eds.), *L'Écrit du temps*, p. 68.
[11] Lévinas, interview in Salomon Malka, *Lire Lévinas*, p. 95.
[12] Katz, *O coração distante*, p. 96.
[13] Gilles Deleuze, and Félix Guattari, *What is Philosophy?*, pp. 65-66.
[14] Nasio, *Five Lessons on the Psychoanalytic Theory of Jacques Lacan*, p. 117.
[15] Blanchot, *The Infinite Conversation*, p. 128.

Exodus, Rupture, Transgression: Abraham and Ruth

The Hebrew Bible attributes fundamental importance to man's condition as stranger: "Thou shalt not pervert the judgment of the stranger, nor of the fatherless; nor take a widow's raiment to pledge: But thou shalt remember that thou wast a bondman in Egypt... therefore I command thee to do this thing" (Deuteronomy 24:17-18). The philosopher Bernard Dov Hercenberg, in his *L'Exil et la puissance d'Israël et du monde*, remarks that the Old Testament emphasizes the precedence of a nomadic experience over a sedentary one, and – more importantly – the continuation of the wandering through the desert and the perpetual repetition of an exodus.

It is in this context that Hercenberg places the story of Abraham, patriarch of the Hebrews, and of his Covenant with YHWH, the Stranger of Strangers. Abraham (a name that in Hebrew means "father of multitudes") started, according to an ancient Talmudic interpretation, an anti-idolatry struggle against the civilization of Assur. Abraham becomes a foreigner when he leaves his parents' house and is exiled from Ur, his native land. A man twice alienated, culturally and geographically, Abraham disengages himself from the images of his original culture when he destroys the idols; with his voluntary exile he is geographically alienated as he wanders into desert.

With regard to exile, the story of Abraham diverges from the beginnings of Biblical man: the fall of Adam and Eve from Paradise, Cain's curse and banishment, and the exile of the Babel generation are similar to the exile of Oedipus, who, having acknowledged his own crimes – incest and parricide – was expelled from Thebes. All of these suffered exile as punishment for transgressions. Both in Greek myth and in these Biblical stories there is an element of persecutory unease concerning an act of violence that brought about exile. But, Hercenberg concludes, the fundamental thing is that the history of the patriarch Abraham gives rise to a notion of exile that has no relationship to punishment, but springs from "being confronting itself, from one who has integrated the experience of freedom and opposition and therefore can surpass it. To Abraham God says not only 'Go' but 'Go to thyself.'"[16]

Abraham's exodus turns into a learning of alterity, an experience of otherness. As Lévinas points out, his departure is an act of opposition to the complacency of the Same, for it is an exile which implies the im-

---

[16] On the parallels and contrasts between the story of Oedipus and Biblical myths, cf. Hercenberg, *L'Exil et la puissance d'Israël et du monde*, Chapter VI.

possibility of return.[17] To leave: this is the ethics that may be derived from the Biblical verse that announces the future. "Now the Lord had said unto Abram, Get thee out of thy country, and from thy kindred, and from thy father's house, unto a land that I will shew thee" (Genesis 12:1). This promise, sealed as a Covenant, announced to the patriarch and his offspring a name, the name of *Hebrews*, who in the future would inhabit the Promised Land flowing with milk and honey: "And I will make of thee a great nation, and I will bless thee, and make thy name great; and thou shalt be a blessing" (Gen. 12:2). Abraham is the first Biblical man to hear the word *stranger*: "Know of a surety that thy seed shall be a stranger in a land that is not theirs, and shall serve them" (Gen. 15:13).

The Hebrew words for the people and their language are *'ivri* and *'ivrit*. The Hebrew, in its etymological meaning, is a being of passage (*la'avor*), of rupture (*'averah*), of transgression (*'averah*) and of transmission (*ha'avarah*): all of these words share the root IBR (*'ayin, veth, resh*). The word *'ibriyt'* might also be translated as "the migrant," migration in itself being neither a curse nor a blessing, but simply the specific calling of this people, previous to the construction of any nation or national union. In this way, the Hebrews' experience of wandering, before the exile in the Diaspora, was a condition for the fulfilling of the pact of the Covenant, and the exile simply perpetuated wandering, the experience of what is not identical to itself. The Hebrew is a being of passage, one that migrates and transgresses. To convey the extension of the condition of exile in the history of the people of the Covenant, Blanchot's words are particularly apt:

> There is a truth of exile and there is a vocation of exile; and if being Jewish is being destined to dispersion – just as it is a call for staying without a place, just as it ruins every fixed relation of force with *one* individual, *one* group, or *one* state – it is because dispersion, faced with the exigency of the whole, also clears the way for a different exigency and finally forbids the temptation of Unity-Identity.[18]

In Hebrew, the fact that the verb "to be" cannot be conjugated in the present reinforces the notion of transitoriness expressed by the very root of the word for "Hebrew." "To be" has past and future only, so that man never "*is*" but is always he or she who was or he or she who will be.

---

[17] Cf. Lévinas, *Transcendence et intelligibilité*.
[18] Blanchot, *The Infinite Conversation*, pp. 125-26.

When one reads the Bible one realizes that Biblical man measures and expresses time in relation to the categories of the finished and unfinished: what he or she has seen (past) and what he or she does not see because it is not finished (future). Discussing this conception of time, André Chourraki quotes Paul Valéry: "Man steps into the future walking backwards."[19] To the Hebrew, existence is becoming.

The Bible tells us that even when Abraham arrives in Canaan, the region promised to him and his descendants, he remains fundamentally a foreigner. When his wife Sarah dies and he buys the cave of Machpelah to serve as a burying ground for her and for himself, he says: "I am a stranger and a sojourner with you: give me a possession of a burying place with you, that I may bury my dead out of my sight" (Gen. 23:4). Abraham's speech reveals the foreignness intrinsic to a culture based on the act of a man who chose to alienate himself from his own people (the Chaldeans of Ur) and become forever a stranger. This act is repeated throughout the centuries in the history of exoduses that have characterized the Jewish people: it underscores the fact that for the Hebrews the founding truth is based on separation.[20]

In *Etrangers à nous-mêmes* (*Strangers to Ourselves*), Julia Kristeva suggests that the unceasing repetition of the Jewish people's wandering and nomadism reinforces the Covenant: its prevalent logic is the choice of foreignness – "becoming-Jew"– intrinsic to the pact between YHWH and his people. Quite properly, she emphasizes that the Hebrew Bible is filled with passages that reassert the insistent presence of the figure of the stranger in the myths and laws of the Jewish people. She draws a rigorous list of paradoxes and contradictions involving the figure of the stranger who is on the move in various texts contained in the Book. Thus, while certain Biblical passages affirm the exclusion of the Other – "And I will establish my covenant between me and thee," says Yahweh to Abraham, "and thy seed after thee" (Gen. 17:7) – other passages contain commandments that impose considerateness to strangers, in the name of the memory of the exile experienced by the Chosen People: "Thou shalt neither vex a stranger, nor oppress him: for ye were strangers in the land of Egypt" (Exod. 22:21). These contradictions, which are quite sharp in the Biblical text, are not insurmountable, since the very Covenant that ensures an identity contains

---

[19] Chourraki, "Traduire la Bible," in *L'Écrit du temps*, Marie Moscovici and Jean-Michel Rey (eds.), p. 24.

[20] Cf. Blanchot, *The Infinite Conversation*, p. 126.

the idea of strangeness that dilutes the certainty of it: "Exclusive as it may be, and while basing that exclusiveness on the moral misdeed of those who are despised, the Jewish people's covenant with its God is an outgrowth not of favoritism but of choice founded on ordeal; this implies that, constantly threatened, the covenant is always to be conquered and its object remains the continuous improvement of the chosen."[21]

Submission to the Law of a God that cannot be represented requires the permanent conquest of the ever-changing place of the chosen: "The land is mine; for ye are strangers and sojourners with me" (Lev. 25:23). And the Covenant (*brith*), which, as has been shown, means "cut" in Hebrew, exists solely because it takes place between parties that are fundamentally dissociated. The Covenant "is the contradiction that exists in the joining of what is fundamentally dissociated,"[22] and requires that both parties be inevitably punctual in their exchanges: deconstructions of boundaries in order to seek – in the exterior, in the "outside," in "exile" – the difference, as long as the trait of unshakable faith in the unknowable is preserved.

Ger, one of the Hebrew words for "foreigner" or "stranger," in the Book of Ruth refers to a privileged personage, one who has been chosen on the basis of the Biblical commandment to "love the stranger": "and thou shalt love him as thyself; for ye were strangers in the land of Egypt" (Lev. 19:34). The story of Ruth begins when the family of Elimelech leaves Judah in a time of famine for the foreign reign of Moab. This migration stirs God's wrath, and he sends the angel of death to Elimelech and his male descendants, sparing only his wife, Naomi, and Ruth and Orpah, the Moabite women who had married his sons. Ruth chooses to leave Moab and return with her mother-in-law to Bethlehem: in this way Elimelech's migration will find closure in the feminine alterity of Ruth. When she arrives in the Promised Land, Ruth submits to leviratic law and becomes the wife of Boaz, a close relative of her dead husband, and this union results in a son. So it is that Ruth earns her place in Jewish history as an ancestress of King David, from whose lineage the Messiah will arise.

An inhabitant of that "other scene," which proclaims that there is no completeness or harmony, not even when one is a member of God's Chosen People, Ruth underlies what is most exterior to and most intimate in the people of Israel. A close analysis of this Biblical episode also points

---

[21] Kristeva, *Strangers to Ourselves*, p. 66.
[22] Enriquez, "Un peuple immortel?" in Moscovici and Rey, *L'Écrit du temps*, p. 129.

to the presence of an act of transgression in the origins of the royalty of the Chosen People: the Bible says that Ruth is directly descended from an act of incest. When Sodom was destroyed, Lot and his daughters had incestuous intercourse because they believed they were the only survivors in the world. This transgression resulted in the birth of Moab, whose name means "sprung from the father" and who is a direct ancestor of Ruth. But the Biblical story involving this character does not at all discourage transgression. The very word for "transgression" in Hebrew is built on "the same three letters that described Hebrewness in such phrases as 'Abraham, the Hebrew' or 'Moses, the Hebrew,'"[23] and has contradictory meanings (as do most words in primitive languages). In this way, if to transgress means to break the law, it also means to go beyond: the story of the Moabite woman suggests that the Covenant subordinates the subject to the ethics of reabsorption not only of the stranger but also of transgression and deviation, as long as they may be subordinated to the global design of seeking in difference the contribution of the Other. The Book of Ruth is an uncanny narrative, in the Freudian sense of "uncanny": in addition to pointing to a dynamic of reabsorption of the Other in the condition of the stranger who founded the Covenant, it incorporates transgression and deviation by subordinating them to the global design of seeking in difference the fecundity of Otherness.[24]

Wandering, exile, nomadism, migration, return and solitude, thus refer to radical and primordial openings to the Other, ontologically prior to any identity.[25] The Hebrew tradition of facing the foreign is continued in the age-old exile of the Diaspora, expressing itself in a discourse of contemporary Judaism that attempts to translate the heteronomy of the Law of the Covenant into multiple instances of becoming-Jew.

Jacob's Struggle with the Angel

If German Romanticism was crucial to Freud's formulation of *das Unheimliche*, the uncanny, the Old Testatment was no less so, in its insistence on revealing "a foreign God or… a Foreigner apt to reveal God." To the Biblical signifiers is added Freud's personal history: as a wandering

---

[23] Hercenberg, *L'Exil*, p. 70.
[24] As Kristeva keenly observes in *Strangers to Ourselves*.
[25] Lévinas, *Éthique et infini*.

Jew from Polish Galicia through Diaspora Vienna to London, he "conditions his concern to face the other's discontent as ill-ease in the continuous presence of the 'other scene' within us."[26] If Freud took in stride the Jew's condition as unassimilable stranger, his opting for "citizenship" in this "land of refuge that each of us carries inside"[27] – the unconscious – certainly helped him reiterate his conviction that it was useless to erase differences and dangerous to lose the dimension of the stranger that is found in the archaeology of our memory. A disturbing god, who cannot be represented or named, also suggests the circumstances of an encounter with strangeness. "The disturbing strangeness" would be the most adequate translation for the title of the 1919 essay "Das Unheimliche," ("The Uncanny") in which Freud develops the idea that the unknown is inherent in the subject. A semantic analysis of the German word *unheimlich* takes the reader to a confrontation of opposites. *Heimlich* means what is familiar, but also suggests its opposite: secret, clandestine, strange. Freud remained faithful to the semantic implication of the term: what is strange is a frightening truth, which evokes what is well known and familiar to the subject.

It has long been recognized, in some Biblical stories, that the dialogue between man and his God is a beautiful metaphor with which to discuss the meaning of the subject's encounter with the Unknowable:

> And Jacob was left alone; and there wrestled a man with him until the breaking of the day. And when he saw that he prevailed not against him, he touched the hollow of his thigh; and the hollow of Jacob's thigh was out of joint, as he wrestled with him. And he said, Let me go, for the day breaketh. And he said, I will not let thee go, except thou bless me. And he said unto him, What is thy name? And he said, Jacob. And he said, Thy name shall be called no more Jacob, but Israel: for as a prince hast thou power with God and with men, and hast prevailed. (Gen. 32:24-8)

In the Talmud, Jacob, during his lonely struggle on Penuel, turns into someone else. The moment when God confers the new name of Israel (*yashar-el* means "straight to God") on Jacob (*'aqeb* means "heel," that which is in contact with the soil) and his future descendants, is precisely the moment when Jacob/Israel, uprooted, his feet not planted on the soil, begins to address directly what lies beyond place, home, and being. Ac-

---

[26] Kristeva, *Strangers to Ourselves*, p. 181.
[27] Flem, *Freud the Man: An Intellectual Biography*, pp. 78-79.

cording to Lévinas's reading in *Quatre Lectures talmudiques*, Jacob's "straightness" when he is given the name Israel, names what is stronger than death, the urgency of a destiny that leads to another rather than to an eternal return to oneself.[28] In this way, the "passage" from Jacob to Israel is a sign of an "identity" that, being located beyond the identical, is translated as a movement of absolute directness to an Other and takes shape in an ethical configuration that necessarily implies the relation with an Other.

But who is the Other? The question is asked by Blanchot, who observes that soon after the fight with the Stranger, Jacob meets his brother Esau again and tells him:

> "I have seen thy face, as though I had seen the face of God." What is remarkable about this sentence is that Jacob does *not* tell Esau: "I have just seen God as I now see you," but rather: "I see you as one sees God." This is a confirmation of the wonder of human presence, this Other Presence that is an Other, just as inaccessible, as apart and distant as the Invisible itself, and also a confirmation of what is terrible in an encounter that can result only in recognition or death. He who sees God runs the risk of dying. He who encounters an Other can deal with him only through lethal violence or through the gift of welcoming speech.[29]

According to the tradition, it is thanks to the gift of speech that Jacob was able to face the lethal violence of the Stranger, and in so doing ensured the transmission of the Torah, the "heritage of Jacob's community." In fact, in the face-to-face with the Other, speech is man's weapon; a weapon that, with its power of creation and subjectivization, can overcome fate.

It is in this sense that Harold Bloom, in his attempt to decipher a number of myths from the Bible to the present, observes that Jacob is the most Jewish character in the Book, one who "in every sense primarily means *more life*."[30] To Bloom, Jacob's spirited struggle for life is, par excellence, the meaning of a well-known saying by Spinoza: "Wisdom is not a meditation upon death but upon life." Bloom's reading suggests that Judaism differs from other religions precisely in that it does not meditate upon death. A similar argument may be found in Freud. In the lecture titled "Death and Us," in which he presents his idea that death is unrepre-

---

[28] Lévinas, *Quatre Lectures talmudiques*. See "Deuxième leçon: La Tentation de la tentation."

[29] Blanchot, *The Infinite Conversation*, p. 188.

[30] Bloom, *Ruin the Sacred Truths: Poetry and Belief from the Bible to the Present*, p. 155.

sentable, he calls attention to the fact that in the Hebrew Bible all narratives are concerned with life. "It is very remarkable that our Holy Scriptures have taken no account of this human need for a guarantee of continued existence. On the contrary, at one point it is said: 'Only the living praise God.'"[31] Freud points out Judaism's uniqueness in generating no illusions about life after death.

Jacob's ethos serves Freud as a standard in his discussion of his own struggle with the vicissitudes of the object of psychoanalysis. In *Beyond the Pleasure Principle* he invokes the state of this Biblical character quoting the German Romantic poet Friedrich Rückert: "What we cannot reach flying we must reach limping."[32] In this same passage, Freud tells his imaginary interlocutor that he feels authorized by his scientific curiosity to move *ever onward* and to search for truth and meaning even in poetry and faith. The apparent paradox is that he sought in the metaphor of Jacob's fight with the angel a paradigm that could express the desire that his science might not be taken as a catechism. Freud can surprise the reader by the boldness with which he takes the side of the truth of poetry and the Bible against their denigration by positivist science.

"When breath threatened to fail me in the struggle I prayed the angel to desist, and that is what he has done since then. But I did not turn out to be the stronger, though since then I have been noticeably limping. Well, I really am forty-four now, a rather shabby old Jew."[33] Freud's use of the term "limping" conveys the intrinsic difference of a theory "cooked on a slow fire." His Biblical allusion expresses his desire – the analyst's desire – to persist in the encounter with the unknown.

The most poignant allusion to Jacob in Freud's writings is to be found in the letter he wrote to his son Ernst a few days before he left for London: "I sometimes compare myself with the old Jacob who, when a very old man, was taken by his children to Egypt.... Let us hope that it won't also be followed by an exodus from Egypt. It is high time that Ahasuerus came to rest somewhere."[34] Reduced to his "London-Egypt" exile,

---

[31] Freud, "Death and Us" in *Freud and Judaism*, ed. David Meghnagi.

[32] *SE*, vol. 18, p. 84, n. 1. [*Beyond the Pleasure Principle*]

[33] Freud to Fliess, May 7, 1900, *The Origins of Psycho-Analysis*, pp. 318-9.

[34] Letter dated May 12, 1938, *Letters of Sigmund Freud*. The (post-Biblical) legend of the Wandering Jew – unlike the stories of Abraham, Ruth, and Jacob, in which migration is a search for diversity, a movement toward becoming an Other – involves wandering as a curse. Ahasuerus is the metaphor of one who has been excluded and, by imposition of the Other, is fated to being constantly on the move.

Freud conveys in *Der Mann Moses und die monotheistische Religion* his final reflections on the nature and the destiny of Jewish wandering.

This is the closing of the circle, to refer to Nasio's notion that exile is the goal of analysis. Nasio remarks that in his own personal experience, "exile from oneself constitutes a kind of cure."[35] Nasio's Lacanian orientation encourages him to translate Freud's famous aphorism *Wo Es war, soll Ich werden* as follows: *Ich* stands for "subject," and *Es* for "the most intimate and yet the strangest thing in our being." Therefore we should read: Where the most intimate and yet the strangest thing in our being was, there the subject shall be. The encounter with the *Es,* Nasio argues, can only take place in the exceptional experience of exile from oneself.[36]

It would not be unreasonable to say that the psychoanalytic experience offers an open space to the subject, in which one may experience exile, inventing oneself as an Other, turning to the non-identical. This adventure takes place in the "country of the Other" – that is, somewhere beyond the similar, the identical, and the already known. Abraham's story, his journey in the land of Otherness, is a metaphor for the psychoanalytic journey.

Strangers of the Ego and of the Other: Freud's Moses

It would be impossible to ignore the attempts at assimilation and the cosmopolitanism of most Jewish intellectuals living in Vienna in the early twentieth century. As mentioned in the first chapter, the Jewish intelligentsia attempted in every possible way to make the best of the favorable political moment, and thereby find a definitive haven after the inexorable, age-old exile of the Jewish people. As emancipation and assimilation progressed, some Jews redefined their own Jewishness positively or negatively. And it was precisely at the moment when politically organized anti-Semitism and contemporary state nationalism were taking shape, confident of possessing exact knowledge of what a Jew was, that Viennese modernity gave ample testimony that there is no such thing as *the* Jew, but rather a bewildering multiplicity of constructions of Jewishness.

Prominent among the most recent attempts to understand how this took place is Le Rider's contribution, inspired by Paul Ricœur's theses in

---

[35] Nasio, *Five Lessons*, p. 118.
[36] Ibid.

Time and Narrative about identity as a continuous process of construction. On the basis of Ricœur's analyses of the constitution of identity as a narrative operation, Le Rider attempts to demonstrate how the crisis of identity in modernity led Jews to redefine what a Jew was through writing.

> What the fates of Sigmund Freud, Theodor Herzl, Karl Kraus and Richard Beer-Hofmann have in common is the astonishing freedom with which these intellectuals tried to define what "the Jew" is in the era of assimilation, anti-Semitism and Zionism.... For each of them, Jewish identity formulates, in fictional form, a grand narrative, in which intimate history and the personal unconscious are just as important as the history of the Jewish people or the texts of the religious tradition.[37]

But the problem of Jewish identity cannot be reduced to the crisis of Viennese modernity; in fact, it is much older than that, if Jewishness is taken as the expression of an age-old wandering, a multiplied alterity, torn into shreds. In Vienna, after a long period of assimilation, the Jew sought in the ancient practice of his forebears' writing experience a strategy to elaborate mourning. Since the destruction of the Temple and the expulsion from Jerusalem, Jews have been engaged in the practice of enduring and surviving the experience of deterritorialization by means of the writing of history. The Book, the permanent support of writing, gathers together its people in the Diaspora. Freud's *Der Mann Moses und die monotheistische Religion* belongs in this lineage of writing mentioned by Le Rider: it derives from the relation between one more exodus of the Jewish people and the Jewishness of its author. Freud began to write it approximately one year after many of his books had been burned in Berlin bonfires.[38] The writing of this text bears the indelible mark of the connection between the history of its author and the history of psychoanalysis – a connection that, in

---

[37] Le Rider, *Modernité viennoise*, pp. 11-12.

[38] On May 11th, 1933, Freud wrote in his diary that the night before, following Goebbels orders, the University had organized a series of rituals that involved burning books. More that 20 thousand books were thrown to the fire while one of the students recited against the "written works by non-Germans" dividing them in four categories. At a certain moment one student who had books in his hands classified as fourth category screamed: "Against the exaggeration of the instinctive life that destroys the soul, the nobility of the human soul! I deliver to the flames the writings of Sigmund Freud". (*The Diary of Sigmund Freud - 1929/1939: a chronicle of events in the last decade*). In his biography, Jones had registered the Freud's commentary of this event: "What progress we are making. In the Middle Ages they would have burned me. Now they are content to burning my books". (Jones, *Life and Works*, v. 3, p.118)

the afterward to his autobiography, Freud himself authorizes, as long as it is associated with his discoveries and the transmission of psychoanalysis. The links between the histories of Judaism, of psychoanalysis and Freud himself, are evident in the very first lines of the book: "To deprive a people of the man they take pride in as the greatest of their sons is not a thing to be gladly or carelessly undertaken, least of all by someone who is himself one of them."[39]

In this traumatic statement Freud confesses his intent to stand apart, dispossess, disidentify. The consequences of his confession are felt throughout the narrative of his "historical novel," which takes shape as a "theoretical fiction" built on references to the Pentateuch.[40] Contrary to what many think, *Der Mann Moses und die monotheistische Religion* is not the simple application of Freud's ideas on the father of the horde, first laid out in *Totem and Taboo*. It is a hypertext whose writing cannot be easily captured: multiple, not arbitrary, meanings pop up on every page. Like a puzzle, it is open to various levels of understanding. Although some commentators of Freud read it as an anthropological, psychological, or sociological study, it is in fact a major psychoanalytic text in which the author thoroughly reconfigures his "witch," metapsychology.[41] Making use of a Biblical metaphor, he bequeaths his testament to future generations of analysts. The wandering in the desert, nomadism, the Book and the Law of the Jewish people, guided Freud's pen during his exodus to London; he found in this experience a metaphor with which to speak, between the lines of his "historical novel," of the errancy of the subject. The writing of *Der Mann Moses und die monotheistische Religion* accompanied its author's exodus from Vienna to London. It represents a profound reflection on the fate of psychoanalysis and the preservation of its transmission. It is a trustworthy testimony to the issues that arise on the frontiers surrounding the "land of psychoanalysis": the text contains some reflections on the inevitable clash between science and religion, ethics and worldview, clinical practice and other therapies. Foreign to all, psychoanalysis is unceasingly seeking its legitimacy as a unique method that makes the subject speak about his or her truth.[42]

---

[39] *SE*, vol. 23, p. 7. [*Moses and Monotheism*]

[40] In *Letters of Sigmund Freud and Arnold Zweig*, Freud on Feb, 21, 1936 and Sep. 30, 1934, tells his friend that the book he was writing was to be called *Der Mann Moses, ein historischer Roman* (The Man Moses, a Historical Novel).

[41] *SE*, vol. 23, p. 225. ["Analysis Terminable and Interminable"]

[42] Lacan remarked on these formulations in the 1938 text. In his seminar on *The Ethics of*

It is possible to read Freud's *Der Mann Moses und die monotheistische Religion* from a political perspective; it is his answer to the question he asked Arnold Zweig about barbarity. "Faced with the renewed persecutions," he wrote, "one asks oneself again how the Jew came to be what he is and why he has drawn upon himself this undying hatred."[43] Freud denounces the religious structure of the anti-Semitic totalitarianism that, out of hatred, created a lethal hostility toward the Other. He was no longer alive by the time the Nazis announced the "Final Solution" but he lived long enough to realize that an evil fate awaited the Jews. A letter from Zweig acknowledges Freud's foresight and his understanding of the Nazi plan to eliminate the Jews: "You and no one else restrained me from the folly of returning to Eichkamp, i.e., to the concentration camp and death."[44]

With the rise of Nazism, Freud was confronted with the equation of the experience of being a Jew to that of being a foreigner. In *Der Mann Moses und die monotheistische Religion* foreignness refers to the Jew's status: a stranger unto himself and a stranger unto the other.

The point of departure for Freud's analysis is the idea that Moses, the man who created and founded the Mosaic religion, was in fact an Egyptian. His hypothesis that the founder of Judaism was a foreigner was not entirely novel. In the history of culture this theory already had many proponents, including some figures of the Enlightenment who saw Moses as an *Aufklärer*.[45] In fact, in *Der Mann Moses und die monotheistische Religion* Freud engages the work of Ed. Meyer, an important contemporary historian who had understood Moses to be an Egyptian. From the viewpoint of Judaism, it cannot be said that Freud's idea is contrary to the spirit of the Book of Books and of the Talmud: making Moses a foreigner is in keeping with Biblical ethics. In fact, in Jewish doctrine the thesis that Moses was Egyptian was not unheard of: in the Zohar, one of the medieval kabbalistic books that arose from interpretation of the Torah, Moses appears as an Egyptian, a man who revealed infinity by means of the differential writing of the word YHWH – "My servant Moses is not so.... With him will I speak mouth to mouth, even apparently, and not in dark speeches" (Num. 12:7-8). The Covenant between the Jewish people and God contains in its essence

---

Psychoanalysis (lesson XIII, "The Death of God"), he discusses some of the impasses of the transmission, formation and desire of the analyst in light of *Der Mann Moses und die monotheistische Religion*.

[43] Freud to Arnold Zweig, September 30, 1934, in *The Letters of Sigmund Freud*, pp. 421-422.

[44] Letter of February 15, 1936 in *The Letters of Signund Freud & Arnold Zweig*, pp. 120-21.

[45] Le Rider, *op.cit.*, p. 291.

the original foreign condition of the Chosen People, whose ethos is based on the wandering of strangers toward a future, prior to any sedentary existence.

Indeed, Moses' status as a stranger in Jewish culture was already familiar to Freud. Long before he began writing *Der Mann Moses und die monotheistische Religion*, in one of his *Introductory Lectures on Psychoanalysis* he tells a joke: "There is a well-known comic anecdote according to which a clever Jewish boy was asked who the mother of Moses was. He replied without hesitation: 'The Princess.' 'No,' he was told, 'she only took him out of the water.' 'That's what *she* says,' he replied, and so proved that he had found the correct interpretation of the myth."[46] Freud saw wit as a formation of the unconscious; by telling this curious Jewish joke, he indicated that it contained a fragment of truth that had not been captured by official knowledge

In reading/rewriting the Book of Exodus, Freud attempts to clarify it much as the joke does: by seeking a different truth, beyond the boundaries of repression and censorship. Freud wants to affirm the unsaid, to uncover what has been suppressed, to give voice to the excluded. Like a Talmudist navigating between the blanks and following the wandering of the letters in the Book of Books, he produces a new meaning for the adventure of Moses and his people in the desert. Facing general misunderstanding, Freud insists on "depriv[ing] a people of the man they take pride in as the greatest of their sons," in order to demonstrate that Judaism is the product of a construction that takes place through the experience of foreignness. This is a daring thesis. On the one hand, it wounds the religious feelings of the Jewish people by depriving them of their greatest prophet; on the other hand, it is thoroughly founded on the imperative of the Covenant: to be he who, coming from outside and seeking what is external, testifies against the idea of a fixed, unchanging meaning for the figure of the Jew.[47]

The thesis that Moses was an Egyptian expresses most radically the Biblical conception of what it is to be Jewish, which forces the subject to face radical decentering. The best expression of this is the story of the

---

[46] *SE*, vol. 15, p. 147 [*Introductory Lectures on Psycho-Analysis*]. According to James Strachey, editor of the English-language *Standard Edition* of Freud's works, the construction of *Der Mann Moses und die monotheistische Religion* is derived from the logic behind this joke.

[47] Elie Wiesel describes this disturbing choice of foreignness in his short essay "Why write" in *Confronting the Holocaust: The Impact of Elie Wiesel*, eds. Alvin H. Rosenberg and Irving Greenberg, pp. 200-206.

king who knows he is himself a stranger. "For how long are they to speak to me wrathfully, saying: is he not of unworthy lineage? Is he not a descendant of Ruth the Moabite?" asks an anguished King David of YHWH.[48]

As Yerushalmi points out, "Freud insists, as does the Bible, that the Jews were chosen, that they were chosen from outside, that it was not the Jews who created their religion: it was religion that created the Jews."[49] In a letter of Jan. 6, 1935 to Lou Andreas-Salomé, Freud observes that the logic behind the idea of a chosen people relies on the Hebrews' adoption of a new religion brought by a foreigner. Moses, the Egyptian, invents the Jew; therefore every Jew is an "Egyptian," beyond race and identity. Moses the Egyptian introduces a concept of God whose presence is defined by a radical, absolute absence and by an ethics that leads to the transcendence of idolatry.[50]

To denaturalize and expropriate an ancestral figure of one's own symbolic universe does not necessarily imply self-hatred; rather, it may indicate that one is courageous enough to get rid of a myth in order to integrate new knowledge concerning one's origin, and in this way to construct one's identity. With the publication of *Der Mann Moses und die monotheistische Religion,* Freud, like the prophet, becomes a breaker of idols: he reactivates the Biblical imagination, shatters its greatest idol, and grounds the history of the Jewish people in their relation to foreignness.

In the 1920s Freud drew the parallel between the structure of group organizations and the Ego. Organizations make units that tend to exclude the Other in order to strengthen the identical. As an organized system, religion appeared to Freud as a spiritual idolatry, which gains strength by providing answers in the face of the unknown, veiling existential truths.

---

[48] A Midrashic comment on the Book of Ruth quoted by Julia Kristeva in *Strangers to Ourselves,* p. 74.

[49] See Yerushalmi, *Freud's Moses,* Chapter 2. According to this historian, Freud's reading turns against secular Jewish liberalism, which thought Judaism was the product of the "Jewish genius."

[50] See Jacques Lacan, "The Names of the Father" in *Television,* pp. 81-95. One must underscore the unpardonable mistake of those authors who read *Der Mann Moses und die monotheistische Religion* as the expression of Freud's hatred of his own Jewishness. According to Le Rider (*Modernité viennoise,* p. 294), Paul Roazen in his *Freud, Political and Social Thought* regards the fact that the creator of psychoanalysis denies Moses' Jewishness as irrefutable proof that he suffered from the syndrome of "Jewish self-hatred" (*jüdischer Selbsthass*) common among the Jews in pre-Hitler Europe. This kind of reading is unfounded and is denied by Freud's own statements. On Freud's scathing criticism of Theodor Lessing's account of the "syndrome" of self-hatred see Jones, *Life and Works,* vol. 3, pp. 159-60.

Yet, later on, he corrects his position: "In *The Future of an Illusion* I expressed an essentially negative valuation of religion. Later, I found a formula which did better justice to it: while granting that its power lies in the truth it contains, I showed that this truth was not a material one but a historical one."[51] As Lacan observed, it was necessary for Freud to dissociate the invention of God from the phenomenon of religiosity and the political issue of religious institutions, before he could understand why it was impossible for human beings not to think about the *ex-istence*[52] of God. One might say that the complexity of *Der Mann Moses und die monotheistische Religion* gives a surprising new twist to the psychoanalytic reading of the idea of God. By introducing the notion of historical truth, seeing it as a multiplicity of traits and inscriptions that are incessantly and differentially re-actualized, Freud sees God as a textual operation.[53]

In his investigation of the hatred human beings experience when faced with the difference of others, Freud boldly asserts that the violence to which his own people has been subjected cannot be dealt with from the victim's point of view exclusively. On the contrary, he acknowledges that there is a "demonic" element hidden in everyone, victims and victors alike. In a letter to the writer Romain Rolland in which he identifies the effects of the history of Jewish segregation on his own writings, Freud observes that destructive impulses belong to mankind:

---

[51] *SE*, vol. 21, p. 72. [*The Future of an Illusion*]

[52] Lacan uses the concept of *ex-istence* to confer a unique status to the notion of *existence* and also to refer to the eccentric place of the subject of the unconscious. To express this concept he coins the term *ex-time*, which conjoins *ex-* and *intime* ("intimate") to speak about the articulation of the inside with the outside. This neologism, which aims to account for what is most intimate in the subject and at the same time is exterior to it, best captures the topology of disquieting foreignness: a region exiled in the interior of the subject. "Ex-timate" would be the equivalent English word. In his seminar on the Real, the Symbolic, and the Imaginary, Lacan notes that the question of the *ex-istence* of God is intrinsically associated with the relation between science and the real. Cf. Lacan, unpublished seminar of 1974-75. See Lacan, Seminar 22, *RSI* (1974-75), privately published.

[53] On this topic, see de Certeau, *The Writing of History*, and the three-volume work *Freud et Moïse: Écritures du Père* in which François Balmé, Brigitte Lémere, and Solal Rabinovitch, on the basis of Lacan's elaborations on the different registers of paternity in terms of its complex function, reread the issues presented in *Der Mann Moses und die monotheistische Religion* about what religion has taught us to evoke. The hints in Freud's letter to Fliess of Dec. 6, 1896, in which he represents the unconscious as writing, show clearly how the myth of *Totem and Taboo* pervades all of Freud's work, through his final book of 1939, when it becomes the very letter of the writing of the text itself.

I, of course, belong to a race which in the Middle Ages was held responsible for all epidemics and which today is blamed for the disintegration of the Austrian Empire and the German defeat. Such experiences have a sobering effect and are not conducive to make one believe in illusions. A great part of my life's work... has been spent [trying to] destroy illusions of my own and those of mankind. But if this one hope cannot be at least partly realized, if in the course of evolution we don't learn to divert drives from destroying our own kind, if we continue to hate one another for minor differences and kill each other for petty gain, if we go on exploiting the great progress made in the control of natural resources for our mutual destruction, what kind of future lies in store for us?[54]

To understand the hatred for the other throughout the paradigm of the Jew, the ancestral *unheimlich* of the group was one of the motives behind the writing of *Der Mann Moses und die monotheistische Religion*. Freud had no intention of making Judaism "responsible" for anti-Semitism. Against the grain of nineteenth-century psychiatric and psychological discourse concerning the "degeneracy" of Jews, Freud never came close to blaming Jews for their own fate. Rather, he was interested in analyzing the effects of Jewish uniqueness vis-à-vis the Other.

The careful reader cannot fail to notice that Freud wished to locate the discussion of anti-Semitism in the context of the *narcissism of minor differences*, as the direct effect of a segregationist logic: "In some respects [Jews] are not fundamentally different from their 'host' nations.... And the intolerance of groups is often, strangely enough, exhibited more strongly against small differences than against fundamental ones."[55] Even when discussing the origin of segregation and racism on the basis of Jewish difference, Freud ultimately maintains that Jew-hating, racism, and segregation were undeniably an aggressive reaction of the subject to the difference of another who was extraordinarily close and familiar. Clearly, what is in

---

[54] Letter of March 4, 1923, *Letters of Sigmund Freud*, pp. 341-42. In the light of *Civilization and Its Discontents*, the theoretical implications of this letter to Romain Rolland become clearer. In *Civilization*, where Freud applies the hypothesis of a death drive or destructive drive to culture, he unequivocally states that human nature is basically destructive: "For 'little children' do not like it when there is talk of the inborn human inclination to 'badness,' to aggressiveness and destructiveness." *SE*, vol. 21, p. 120. [*Civilization and Its Discontents*].

[55] *SE*, vol. 23, pp. 90-91. [*Moses and Monotheism*]. Freud's essential discussion of the effects of the other's minor differences on the homogeneous majority is to be found in *Civilization and Its Discontents*, *SE*, vol. 21, p. 3. See also, in the same text, p. 114, where Freud discusses the slaughter of Jews by fraternal communities bound by love, in the light of the narcissism of minor differences.

question here is not just any difference, but one that causes anxiety in the subject. *Ex*-timate difference: abhorrence of what is most intimate, of what, when taken by the ego as an external object, turns into an object of hatred. In the context of this interpretation, the discourse of the German *Führer* is exemplary, for it shows clearly that the Jew was both what was most intimate in himself and most foreign to him: a strange stranger. "The Jew dwells inside us; but it is easier to fight him in his bodily form then as an invisible demon,"[56] Adolph Hitler once confided to Hermann Rauching.

According to Freud, anti-Semitism in modernity encouraged the segregation of Jews by configuring them as non-identical to the National-Socialist mass: "Neither was it an unaccountable chance that the dream of a Germanic world-dominion called for anti-Semitism as its complement."[57] This statement was based on the ideas developed in *Group Psychology and the Analysis of the Ego*: the mass, when enthralled by the fascinating games of identification with the leader, persecutes others encouraged by the belief in the hegemony of the ego. Freud's arguments about segregation as grounds for isolating what is Other are analyzed in depth in *Der Mann Moses und die monotheistische Religion*, where he underscores the notion that the community feeling of masses requires hostility toward the non-identical.

Among the "reasons" for hatred of Jews, Freud mentions an item he identifies as a direct product of the imposition of Christianity by means of strong oppression. He hypothesizes that this coercion, though it took place in the remote past, is still operative in modernity. It seems clear that many of the converted

> have not got over a grudge against the new religion which was imposed on them; but they have displaced the grudge on to the source from which Christianity reached them.... The hatred of the Jews is at bottom a hatred of Christianity, and we need not be surprised that in the German National-Socialist revolution this intimate relation between the two monotheistic religions finds such a clear expression in the hostile treatment of both of them.[58]

What were the irreducible differences of Judaism, which according to Freud were the catalysts of anti-Semitic hatred? Since the late nineteenth

---

[56] Quoted in Armand Zaloszcyc, "Remarques sur la ségrégation constitutive du juif dans le nazisme," *La Lettre* no. 2, 1993.

[57] *SE*, vol. 21, p. 114. [*Civilization and Its Discontents*]

[58] *SE*, vol. 23, pp. 91-92. [*Moses and Monotheism*]

century, the image of the circumcised penis, seen as altered, damaged, or incomplete, had been at the center of the definition of the Jew. Most of the fantasies that would later feed the fires of anti-Semitism converged on the idea that circumcision was a process of feminization of the Jewish male, which left his sex organ degenerate and extremely vulnerable to sexually transmitted diseases. Gilman's studies of medical and social discourse in fin-de-siècle Austrian culture underline that the body of the Jew was seen in highly derogatory and paranoid terms: the degeneracy of Jewish males brought about by circumcision was correlative to their feminization.

In her study of figures of alterity in Viennese culture, Cristine Buci-Glucksmann concludes that the panic over the feminization of European culture since the late nineteenth century was associated with fear of Europe's Judaization. These specters fueled anti-Semitic discourse. Buci-Glucksmann observes that in *Mein Kampf* Hitler emphasized that women's emancipation is an invention of Jews, with their abject desires: "Through the forces of sexual democracy, the Jew steals our women from us."[59] The horror of feminization became the basis of the rhetoric of his political program: "Woman introduced sin in the world... [she] is the primary cause of the pollution of Nordic blood."[60]

It is in the work of Otto Weininger that femininity and Jewishness are most closely related, both being identified with the very spirit of modernity: "In all its aspects, the spirit of modernity is Jewish. Sexuality is celebrated as the supreme value. Our time is not only the most Jewish, but also the most feminine of all."[61] The notion that there was an indissoluble link between femininity and Judaism became widespread among the intelligentsia of *Mitteleuropa*. Freud himself, in his analysis of the Little Hans case, mentions Weininger's ideas:

> The castration complex is the deepest unconscious root of anti-Semitism; for even in the nursery little boys hear that a Jew has something cut off his penis – a piece of his penis, they think – and this gives them a right to despise Jews. And there is no stronger unconscious root for the sense of superiority over women. Weininger (the young philosopher who, highly

---

[59] Buci-Glucksmann, "Figures viennoises de l'alterité. Feminité et judaïté," in Moscovici & Rey, *L'Écrit du Temps,* p. 56.

[60] Quoted in Le Rider, *Modernité viennoise,* p. 216.

[61] Otto Weininger, quoted in Buci-Glucksmann, "Figures viennoises," p. 51. About the excluded figures of the Jew and the woman in Viennese modernity, also see Le Rider, *Modernité viennoise,* passim.

gifted but sexually deranged, committed suicide after producing his remarkable book *Geschlecht und Charakter*), in a chapter that attracted much attention, treated Jews and women with equal hostility and overwhelmed them with the same insults. Being a neurotic, Weininger was completely under the sway of his infantile complexes; and from that standpoint what is common to Jews and women is their relation to the castration complex.[62]

According to Freud, anti-feminism and anti-Semitism share the same phobia of castration, the same horror of the encounter with difference. Circumcision is one of the marks of the Jew's "foreignness." Pointing to absence or privation, circumcision reminds the uncircumcised of the failure of the ideal of virility without losses.

In *My Own Private Germany*, Eric L. Santner emphasizes that for Freud Jewish monotheism and the historical situation of the Diaspora are related to a number of cuts and losses, renunciations and mournings. Century after century, Jews had to deal with traumatic events that cannot be conveyed in language. The ongoing experience of geographical displacement and renunciation became a sort of negative sign for those who insisted on totalitarian projects. In a chapter in which he discusses the Jewish question in the case of Schreber, Santner attempts to demonstrate that this judge's psychological breakdown, documented in his *Memoirs of My Nervous Illness*, was in fact an attempt to avoid the totalitarian temptation that was beginning to take hold of Germany – and which so many Germans after him were unable to resist – by slowly metamorphosing into a woman and merging with the figure of the Wandering Jew. Considering the historical context and the cultural landscape Schreber inhabited, Santner proposes that the nervous breakdown he experienced was a crisis of investiture. On the basis of Freud's contributions to an understanding of modern anti-Semitism, he concludes that Schreber "discovered that his own symbolic power and authority as a judge – and German man – was founded, at least in part, by the performative magic of the rights of institutions, that his sym-

---

[62] *SE*, vol. 10, p. 36. ["Analysis of a Phobia in a Five-Year-Old Boy"]. Discussing sex in the texts of Talmudic culture, Boyarin (*"'This We Know to Be the Carnal Israel': Circumcision and the Erotic Life of God and Israel," Critical Inquiry* 18) affirms that the representation of the male as woman was not just an external fantasy of anti-Semites but also a representation internal to Judaism: according to rabbinical interpretations, circumcision is seen as feminizing the male, making him receptive for the encounter with the divine. According to Boyarin's reading, in direct contrast with the anti-Semitic contention that circumcision is bodily mutilation, Jewish texts repeatedly emphasize the symbolic aspect of this mark: *being a man means to pass through femininity*.

bolic function was sustained by an imperative to produce a regulated series of repeat performances" that were "idiotic." Compulsion at the heart of the symbolic was felt by Schreber as an injunction to cultivate *jouissance*. The sexualization that Schreber experienced as "feminizing and 'Jewifying', Santner adds, suggests that at the advent of European modernity 'knowledge' of *jouissance* was ascribed to women and Jews." Both occupied "the place of that which could not be directly acknowledged: that symbolic identities, are, in the final analysis, sustained by *drive*, by performativity-as-repetition-compulsion."[63]

Jews' contention that they are God's firstborn and chosen people has forever roused hatred toward them. Freud demonstrates that the idea of a chosen people, strategically introduced by Moses the Egyptian, is powerfully shared in the form of envy and jealousy by non-Jews. "It is as though they had thought there was truth in [the Jews'] claim" of being chosen.[64] Hitler's discourse seems to substantiate Freud's insight: "There can be no two chosen peoples," states the *Führer*, "*we* are God's people."[65]

Finally, among the differences that make the Jew the stranger, Freud gives primary importance to one characteristic inscribed in the very structure of the Jewish religion, and which summarily disqualifies it as an universal religion: the nonrecognition of the original murder of the Father.[66] Earlier, Freud had already stressed this same structural aspect of Jewish monotheism, which – together with Jews' refusal to use religion to produce comforting illusions about life and death – makes Judaism a disquieting and unnerving religion.[67]

In the absence of a Jewish religious ritual representing the violence against the Father, Freud recognizes a reason for ascribing the murder of God to the Jews. According to Freud the Jews, not having accepted the murder of the father, took "a tragic load of guilt on themselves; they have

---

[63] Eric L. Santner, *My Own Private Germany: Daniel Paul Schreber's Secret History of Modernity*, pp. 122 and 124-25.

[64] *SE*, vol. 23, p. 115. [*Moses and Monotheism*]

[65] Quoted by Jean-Joseph Goux, *El inconsciente freudiano y la revolución iconoclasta*, p. 54.

[66] *SE*, vol. 23, p. 75. [*Moses and Monotheism*]. Freud attempted to account for the universality of Oedipal prohibitions by constructing a myth: he imagined that one day the sons had killed the primordial father (*Ur-vater*) and devoured him; this event was the beginning of the course of civilization, based on primordial guilt. The totem is then the expression of this lack, raised to the status of surrogate father. Seen as protecting ancestor, the totem was also jointly killed and eaten by the members of the tribe, in a celebration of the sons' victory.

[67] Freud, "Death and Us," in *Freud and Judaism*, ed. David Meghnagi.

been made to pay heavy penance for it."[68] The empty place of the Father, ensured as such by the ban against the representation of God, differentiates Judaism from Christianity, which attempts to redeem man through the death of the Son of God. By acceding to what had been abandoned by the Jews – the representation of the murdered Father – Christianity became a universal religion.

Freud identifies the effect of this lack of recognition of the murder of the father in the anti-Semitism that in his own time promoted segregation. In his correspondence with Arnold Zweig Freud makes clear that he knows how flimsy are his hypotheses founded on the researches of E. Sellin, who contended that Moses had been murdered by his people. Yet, Freud carries out his project of analyzing the history of Judaism on the basis of the myth constructed in *Totem and Taboo*. He asks himself what is the difference between the Jewish group formation and the huge modern masses that manifestly and directly enact the model of the horde, the murder and the love of the Father.[69] Such is the condition of the Jew: he permanently calls into question the other's and his own identity in a permanent return to the desert: the return of Abraham (the Hebrew, the man of passage), of Ruth the Moabite (the foreign matriarch of Jewish royalty), of Jacob/Israel (who struggles with the Angel of the Foreign God) and of Moses the Egyptian (who, being an other, calls himself a Jew).

This brings to mind Blanchot's observation concerning the notion of *responsibility*: the Jews are not different from others, contrary to what racists want to persuade everyone else of: they simply act as living reminders of the requirement of foreignness.[70] It is also this requirement that the psychoanalyst may take up in order to acknowledge Freud's ethical innovation as an atheist.

---

[68] *SE*, vol. 23, p. 136. [*Moses and Monotheism*]

[69] In *Group Psychology and the Analysis of the Ego* Freud claims that the Church and the Army are artificial masses that acquire and preserve their power as long as the individuals place a single object, the same for all, in the place left vacant by the dead Father, and identify themselves not only with one another but also, and most importantly, with this same beloved and idealized object. This essay, according to Paul-Laurent Assoun (in "El sujeto del ideal, aspectos del malestar en la cultura," p. 109) reveals how the Freudian myth of the primitive horde is enacted today.

[70] Blanchot, *The Infinite Conversation*, p. 129.

Chapter 4
YHWH, the Stranger of Strangers

All the letters make up absence. Thus God is the son of His name.

EDMOND JABÈS [1]

The degree of foreignness experienced by the Jewish people is correlative to the strength and intensity of the second commandment of Mosaic Law: "Thou shalt not make unto thee any graven image, or any likeness of any thing that is in heaven above, or that is in the earth beneath, or that is in the water under the earth" (Exod. 20:4). Many thinkers have pondered the strangeness of this law, emphasizing its effects on culture or making use of it to elaborate their own ideas. To examine this commandment and its relation to the development of alterity in Judaism, it will be necessary to examine what some of these thinkers have written.

Let us begin with George Steiner's provocative reflections in an attempt to locate precisely the impact that this Mosaic commandment, together with the spelling of the unpronounceable Tetragrammaton – YHWH, the sign of the presence of the Jewish God – had on the human mind. Steiner writes: "The God of the Torah not only prohibits the making of images to represent Him. He does not allow imagining. His attributes are, as Schoenberg concisely expressed them in *Moses und Aron*, 'Inconceivable because invisible; / because immeasurable; / because everlasting; / because eternal; / because omnipresent; / because omnipotent'."[2] The conclusions drawn by historians of religion concerning the invention of monotheism lead Steiner to state that these attributes imposed and still impose Absence on the human mind, which is constantly trying to organize itself toward images and the figured presence. What is clear, Steiner observes, is that this strange invention continues to haunt Western culture with its requirement of absolute transcendence of human consciousness,

---

[1] Quoted in Derrida, *Writing and Difference*.
[2] Steiner, *In Bluebeard's Castle: Some Notes Towards the Redefinition of Culture*, p. 37.

and does so in such a way that Western man has come to nourish feelings of profound hatred and murderous resentment directed at those who invented the presence of this radical Absence.³

The astounding strangeness of a God made of nothing, with no content, no name, and no essence, is the scandal of radical alterity, of an absence without limit in time, an absence yesterday, today, and forever. Similarly, the unsayable Name of the Hebrew Bible is what is radically outside-of-discourse, what is in the order of language but cannot be fixed – that is, contained in an identity. The strictly unthinkable and unassimilable God, transparent as desert air, to use Steiner's phrase, is entirely different from other forms of human religious expression, from the totem to the Christian Trinity: its status is of another order.

On Hebrew Iconoclasm

Immanuel Kant is one of the philosophers who have investigated the Mosaic idea of God's unrepresentability. Kant points to the link between his conception of the sublime – the experience of the impossibility of reaching the Thing (*das Ding*)⁴ – and the second commandment, which states that God cannot be represented without disfigurement of the inaccessible character of his nature. In his *Critique of Judgment* Kant observes that the second commandment, as the most sublime passage in the Old Testament, in itself is enough to explain "the enthusiasm which the Jewish people, in their moral period, felt for their religion when comparing themselves with others."⁵ Kant also emphasizes the effects of this prohibi-

---

³ Steiner's thesis, as formulated, is a fundamental contribution to the study of the horror of World War II: the Holocaust is a reflex of urges of perverse polytheism and animism, whereby killing the Jews would eliminate the spokesmen of the intolerable Absence of God. See Steiner, *op. cit.*, Chapter 2.

⁴ *Das Ding*, in current parlance, refers to what may be thought, supposed, denied, or affirmed; in the theory of knowledge, the Thing is opposed to the phenomenon and, in this sense, may be taken as synonymous with "object"; and in Kantian metaphysics it refers to what subsists in itself and presupposes nothing else. (Cf. Lalande, *Vocabulaire technique et critique de la philosophie*, pp. 136-7). In psychoanalysis, *das Ding* is the absolute object, the lost object of a mythical satisfaction, which the subject's libido indefatigably attempts to find. *Das Ding* is the subject's absolute Other, so that from the very outset it is clear that it can never be found. See Chemama, "(la) Chose" in *Dictionnaire de la Psychanalyse*, pp. 54-56.

⁵ Kant, *The Critique of Judgment*, Corel Co. ed., 159.

tion in Islam, the other religion that adopts in its foundations this characteristic of Mosaic monotheism. For Kant the sublime is directly associated with the Unrepresentable, with what cannot be contained in any sensible form. Enthusiasm, caused by the sublime object, is the negative affect par excellence, the one that arises out of the inadequacy of the faculty of imagination. Enthusiasm ensues when the subject is unable to reach the thing; this is why the authentic sublime, unlike the beautiful, exceeds the measure of the senses and is an aesthetic lesson in what cannot be represented.

What, then, according to Kant, is the relation between the sublime and the law? The answer is to be found at the center of his explanation of how the aesthetic category of the sublime may be associated with the Mosaic scene of a reality that exceeds the senses and imagination: the aesthetic *satisfaction* of the sublime is nourished by respect for the law. To Kant, this respect is the feeling of inadequacy, "the feeling of our incapacity to attain to an idea that is a law for us."[6] The transcendent reach of the sublime lies in the Unrepresentable Being that makes the law, which is tantamount to recognition that reason can never encompass everything.

Like Kant, Freud questions the scope of the Unrepresentable and its relation to the law. When he elaborated his theories about the Jewish religion in *Der Mann Moses und die monotheistische Religion*, he observed that it was precisely the prohibition against representing and pronouncing God's name that had had the effect of sparking off the "characteristic development of the Jewish nature."[7] Evidently, "Jewish nature" – a better name for which might be the "Jewish condition" or, to use a modern term, Jewishness – is by no means something given biologically, but rather what is uniquely built on the basis of the *heteronomy* of the law. Freud's hypothesis is that, under the impact of the "dematerialization of God,"[8] the Jews were forced to develop a tendency toward abstraction, which grew stronger as political misfortunes were heaped on them throughout centuries of exile and exodus. In short, in his interpretation of the creation of monotheism, Freud proposes that the second commandment, imposed by Moses the Egyptian, introduced a radical change in the Hebrew people's relationship to itself and to other peoples, Egyptians included:

---

[6] Ibid., p. 132.
[7] *SE*, vol. 23, p. 115. [*Moses and Monotheism*]
[8] Ibid.

> Among the precepts of the Moses religion there is one that is of greater importance than appears to begin with. This is the prohibition against making an image of God – the compulsion to worship a God whom one cannot see. In this, I suspect, Moses was outdoing the strictness of the Aton religion. Perhaps he merely wanted to be consistent: his God would in that case have neither a name nor a countenance. Perhaps it was a fresh measure against magical abuses. But if this prohibition were accepted, it must have a profound effect. For it meant that a sensory perception was given second place to what may be called an abstract idea – a triumph of intellectuality over sensuality or, strictly speaking, an instinctual renunciation, with all its necessary psychological consequences.[9]

What is striking about this thesis is Freud's observation that faith in the *invisible* implied the progress of *Geistigkgeit* (intellectuality/spirituality)[10]: the law that imposed faith in the invisible exploded man's image of the world, so that the notion of fixed and changeless representation lost its primacy. The notion of a God that was not subsumed into the known and the familiar brought about an emptiness around which Judaism was structured, and this forced the Jewish people to be ever attuned to the Unknowable. Freud says that the demythologizing impact of the second commandment caused a radical change in man's view of the universe, and that science is the direct descendant of the ideas espoused by Moses, the Egyptian, for it involves reading what lies beyond the visible.

The effect of Mosaic law on the constitution of scientific thought has been commented on by different authors. Ernst Cassirer's history of symbolic forms, according to Hercenberg, awards a special place in the development of science to the subversive movement of the prophets, who always found support in the second commandment. The anti-idolatry reaction described in the prophetic books implies man's effort to go beyond the world of myth, which led to new forms of representation and communication between men. Cassirer writes: "All the religious and *ethical* ardor of the prophets... is founded on the will that leads them *beyond* any intuition of the given and of existence pure and simple.... The prohibition of idol-

---

[9] *SE*, vol. 23, pp. 112-13. [*Moses and Monotheism*]

[10] The German word *Geistigkeit* was translated, in the English *Standard Edition* of Freud's works, as "intellectuality," although the most obvious choice would have been "spirituality." The translator avoided it because he felt it might lead to a misreading of Freud's text. See *SE*, vol. 23, p. 114, n. 4. [*Moses and Monotheism*]

atry – that is, representation in an image or portrait of anything in the sky or in the ground, underwater or on land – thus takes on, in the prophetic consciousness, a meaning and a strength that are entirely new."[11]

Hercenberg's reading of Cassirer's idea is invaluable, for he adds that the culture of exile imposed on the Jewish people in its founding was what gave support to Mosaic law and its enforcement. The precedence of the experience of nomadism and wandering over that of permanent settlement favored and encouraged the enforcement of the anti-idolatry law. Propelled by the encounter with differences, science can achieve its aim by preserving the *sense of the infinite* proper to wandering and to the nomadism of language, of affects, and ideas.

In his *Études d'histoire de la pensée scientifique*, Alexandre Koyré shows that it is impossible to neatly separate the history of scientific thought, the history of philosophical thought, and the history of religious thought. Koyré believes that the evolution of trans-scientific, philosophical, metaphysical, and religious ideas is intimately connected with the evolution of scientific thought. If scientific revolutions have taught men to eschew the sacredness of the mythical imagination, this does not imply that these revolutions arose full-fledged and perfect. On the contrary, they were prepared, according to Koyré,[12] within a broader struggle against fixed ideas and the development of the sense of alterity, which led to the collapse of a closed view of the universe. In this process, man was caught up in two movements: that of circumscribing reality with the help of paradigms that allowed him to think about the world and act on it, and that of demolishing the structures that man himself had created so that the new might arise.[13] This mode of apprehending reality has been invaluable not only for the emergence of science but also for its advancement and support, for it keeps scientific thought from closing itself in on its own findings.

The view of God as unknowable and ineffable forced Mosaic doctrine into an iconoclastic injunction, subverted only when new "golden calves" were forged. Iconoclasm is the presence of atheism in the heart of Judaism.

---

[11] Cassirer, quoted in Hercenberg, *L'Exil*, Chapter V.
[12] See Koyré, "De l'influence des conceptions philosophiques sur l'évolution des théories scientifiques," in *Études d'histoire de la pensée scientifique*, pp. 253-69.
[13] See Thomas Kuhn, *The Structure of Scientific Revolutions*, Chapter 4.

In *El inconsciente freudiano y la revolución iconoclasta*, Jean-Joseph Goux discusses the Jewish roots of psychoanalysis, and the problems of transmission in it, precisely in terms of the iconoclastic tendency of Judaism. Goux extends the notion of Hebraic iconoclasm to include the thought of Karl Marx: both psychoanalysis and Marxism, two major iconoclastic revolutions of the Western world, are "legitimate children" of the ancient anti-idolatry struggle of the Hebrews and their prophets. Indeed, one of Goux's central concerns is to demonstrate that Marx and Freud, both following the same tendency of their ancestors, elaborate theories that denounce the fetishistic effects of a world generated by modern forms of idolatry.

Psychoanalysis is built on the recognition of the impossibility of grasping an all-powerful, finite, and exhaustive knowledge. It is a practice that has the curious goal of reaching a "region where representation remains in suspense, on the edge of itself, open, in a sense, to the closed boundary of finitude,"[14] where the "golden calves" are destroyed. This is the effort that forces the analyst to pass through affects and ideas the way nomads cross deserts and cities.

Separation, the Void, and the Word

Although Judaism contains heterogeneity in the myriad readings it is open to, what is most noteworthy about its foundation is that it is ultimately "the expression of a radical divorce between man and the world, of a chasm that opened between man and God."[15]

The Hebrew term for God, *qadosh*, translated as "holy," etymologically means "separate." Lévinas's reading of *qadosh* refers to what is infinitely separated from all that is common, so that "the inscription of the name of God itself would be the original inscription of a difference."[16] What is *qadosh* is atopic, placeless, just as the temple is empty of images and the Name is not to be pronounced.

The separation between God and man introduced into the history of religion the absolute transcendence of God, as Lévinas stresses, pointing out the necessary distinction between the *sacred* and the *holy* in the in-

---

[14] Foucault, *The Order of Things*, p. 374.

[15] Jeanne Defontaine, "Experience culturelle et perte du sens: dé-significations et malaise d'une indifférence."

[16] Lévinas, *Dieu, la mort et le temps*, p. 274.

commensurable Hebrew word that is the Name of God.[17] *Qadosh* refers to an Alterity radically separated and desacralized – that is, without content, without object, and without any associated form, transcendent to the point of Absence. And because it dwells outside space, beyond time, the *holy* will forever be the Stranger of Strangers. Thus the foreignness of the Jewish God is entirely consistent with the foreignness of his people. The word *qadosh*, in Biblical and Talmudic tradition, is an attribute of the deity; yet, it may also be applied to men – *qedoshim* (plural of *qadosh*) in Hebrew – who were made, according to the Biblical story (Gen. 1: 26-27), in the likeness of a God that admits no images. This antinomy – identification with the absence of image – implies that man, being holy and separate, is also irreducible to any fixed and unchanging representation.[18] There is always something that eludes man's own mirroring image.

When one thinks of this unapproachable and transcendental God, distant and absolutely Foreign, as Blanchot observes, one generally stresses solely his absolute Absence, omitting the fact that the revelation of this One Absent God is accompanied by the "revelation of speech as the place where men hold themselves in relation with what excludes all relation: the infinitely Distant, the absolutely Foreign."[19] This comment is relevant and in harmony with the Biblical and Talmudic texts that see the relationship between man and the Stranger of Strangers not as a source of philosophical speculation or mystic or ecstatic experience, but as a term of an ethical foundation that rests on the primacy of the word.

Since Revelation – both the written Torah and the oral Torah – is revelation of the word, it is essentially a "logophony," or, more precisely, a "nomophony," that is, the expression of the *word* as *law*, both being denoted by the single Hebrew word *dabar* (both "word" and "law," since it is God's word). As David Banon explains: "This infinite word... because it cannot be synchronized with the signs that capture it... is inscribed in a narrative and in a law. This inscription will be the trace of a primary, primordial word, of a saying that is already removed from the said."[20] The word is then the infinite thread with which the fabric is woven that covers the unbridgeable void between God and man, between man and man, *qadosh* and *qedoshim*.

---

[17] See in particular *Dieu, la mort et le temps* and *Totality and Infinity*.
[18] See Banon, *La lecture infinie*, pp. 108-9.
[19] Blanchot, *The Infinite Conversation*, p. 127.
[20] Banon, op. cit., p. 33.

The space of separation between God and man is future time, the paradigm of which is given by the "burning bush" episode in Exodus: "And Moses said unto God, Behold, when I come unto the children of Israel, and shall say unto them, The God of your fathers hath sent me unto you; and they shall say to me, What is his name? what shall I say unto them? And God said unto Moses, I will be what I will be" (Exod. 3:13-14).[21] "I will be what I will be" (*'ehiyeh asher 'ehiyeh*), is God's answer to Moses, condensed in the form of the Tetragrammaton *YHWH*, "I will be what I will be."[22] What is contained in the idea of a God that presents Himself without an image and entirely distinct from the world, then, is a time never reached, a continuing future.[23] "I will be what I will be": this is the incisive nature of the Mosaic revelation, which necessarily implicates the people in their own becoming, expectant of their own Other as Other.

If it is possible to distinguish *messianism* from the *messianic*, as Derrida does when he associates the latter with the performative to come – "whose archive no longer has any relation to the record of what is, to the record of the presence of what is or what will have been *actually* present"[24] – one may say that the condition of YHWH is not only not being known but also not being knowable as such, no more than the pure inscription of difference. Derrida introduces the concept of the messianic to underscore that the unique concept of God in the universe of the Old Testament is translated as to-come; the Tetragrammaton must be said in a number of ways, as the experience of the apprehension of the Same that is ever an Other. We concur with Philippe Julien when he says that the notion of a god without a Name is radically different from that of ontotheology, according to which God says "I am he who is" so that the Name itself may finally be apprehended.[25]

YHWH – the writing that can be read only in the unending repetition of an unsayable sound – cannot be taken as a signifier of something lying behind this combination of letters. YHWH cannot be pronounced; it is not the sacrament of conciliation, nor the signifier of some other thing

---

[21] In general, translators of the Hebrew Bible in the West follow the Greek and Latin versions here, using the present tense of "be." I have changed the tense to the future, in accordance with the Hebrew original.

[22] Wigoder (ed.), *Dictionnaire encyclopédique du judaïsme*, p. 316.

[23] de Certeau, *The Writing of History*, p. 341.

[24] Derrida, *Archive Fever*, p. 72.

[25] Julien, *L'Étrange jouissance du prochain: Science, éthique, religion*, p. 118.

hidden behind it; as de Certeau aptly observes, it is a graph that signals language just as circumcision is the graph that marks the Jew's body.[26]

This way of reading the written form of God's name attracted Freud's attention when he elaborated his theory of thought processes in dreams: "Among the ancient Hebrews the name of God was taboo; it might neither be spoken aloud nor written down.... This prohibition was so implicitly obeyed that to this very day the vocalization of the four consonants of God's name (יהוה) remains unknown. It was, however, pronounced 'Jehovah,' being supplied with the vowels of the word 'Adonai' ('Lord'), against which there was no such prohibition."[27] Freud uses the Tetragrammaton as a conceptual figure to show how the latent ideas in the dream can be expressed only through displacements and condensations, up to the "navel" of the dream, where there is always something that eludes the order of discourse, because it cannot be pronounced. The idea of *God as pure letter* expresses the structure of the dream, where figurations must be read as letters.

In his disquieting otherness, YHWH provokes angst. A "sound" in silence, angst arises as an echo of the crossing of the desert, of the inexorable exile one is fated to since birth. YHWH's specificity consists not in being the only God, but in being beyond representation. Any univocal reading of his name is a way to distance oneself from the angst of the void and weave out of language the fabric to cover it, however provisionally.[28]

---

[26] de Certeau, *The Writing of History*, p. 341.

[27] *SE*, vol. 12, p. 341. ["The Significance of Sequences of Vowels"]

[28] On the unrepresentabilty of God see Lacan, *Le Séminaire* X, *L'Angoisse*, XVIII, "La voix de Yahweh," passim. *Le Séminaire, Livre X: L'Angoisse*, 2004. In *Dieu est inconscient* [God is unconscious], a title that directly quotes Lacan's well-known aphorism, François Regnault draws an analogy between the Hebrew conception of YHWH and Freud's conception of the death drive. Regnault uses the Hebrews' unpronounceable Tetragrammaton as an auxiliary representation, in order to speak more precisely about the unknown of the unconscious and the silence of the death drive. His metaphor reaffirms alterity as part of the foundation of both Judaism and psychoanalysis, underlining through language what cannot be said by language.

Betty B. Fuks

Listening to Silence

Jean-François Lyotard's observations on the theory of religion Freud developed in *Der Mann Moses und die monotheistische Religion* emphasize that Mosaic law had the effect of making the visible recede to the legible-audible.[29] The words of the poet will help illustrate this proposition: "Of his people, God demands that they listen: 'Hear, O Israel.' But hear what? Hear the words of your God; but God is absent and his words are voiceless, for their sounds are shut off by distance. Listen to the silence, for it is in this silence that God speaks to his creature. The original prohibition is what makes nonrepresentation sacred. God's language is the language of absence."[30] The prohibition of images is correlative to the importance attributed to sound and the letter. Listening and speaking are the senses that are given pride of place in Jewish liturgy, the major prayer in which is called *Shemah'* or Listening, which begins "Hear, O Israel, the Lord is God, the Lord is One." The Hebrew verb for "listen" (*lishnot*) means simultaneously "listen," "hear," and "obey." The Text is read aloud, and what in the Western world is known as "scripture" in the phrase "Holy Scripture" corresponds in Hebrew to *mikra'*, "reading." The founders of Judaism inaugurated a tradition of reading-writing the Word not as an unveiling of meaning, but rather as creation of meaning.[31] Judaism made the transition from seeing to listening: one does not see a text, but rather reads the letters, or – what amounts to the same thing – "listens" to the succession of the letters, infinitely combining with one another before God's silence. In this sense, one may say that Judaism is the expression of an eye that closed so that the Word might be heard.[32]

Psychoanalysis is certainly tributary to this primacy of listening as an ethical reference and a basis of its clinical method. Historically, psychoanalysis broke with the clinical practice based on sight, which found expression in hypnosis and suggestion, by creating an original tool: free association – the wandering of the letter – for the patient and floating *listening* for the analyst. This break marked the beginning of a new form of clinical practice: to listen to the symptom amounts to finding the plurality of meanings for its sign. Investigation of the formations of the unconscious

---

[29] Lyotard, "Figure forclose. L'Écrit du Temps," *Questions de Judaïsme*, 5 (Winter 1984).
[30] Jabès, "Judaïsme et écriture," in *L'écrit du temps*, p. 8.
[31] Lévinas and Cohen, *Ethics and Infinity: Conversations with Philippe Nemo*.
[32] See Lyotard, "Figure forclose," p. 78.

introduces alterity into the very core of the physician-patient relationship: the presence of the analyst creates a third order between the *I* and *thou* of ordinary dialogue, which redirects the subject toward the actualization of its psychological truth. In this movement lies the difference between psychoanalysis and the other forms of therapies that man has used for centuries to assuage mental pain. The analytical tool is, in this way, akin to the iconoclastic ethics of Mosaic Law, in which man addresses the Nameless in order to understand the nexus of things, and the only audible reply is the echo of his own voice.[33]

---

[33] According to Lacan, the true formula of atheism is not *God is dead* ... the true formula of atheism is *God is unconscious*. This aphorism is close to the reality of *qadosh*, the Stranger of Strangers, pure inscription of the difference which, separated and distant from everything and everyone, is unrepresentable. Lacan follows (perhaps unknowingly) the etymology of the Hebrew word *qadosh* as "separated." He found in such Catholic mystics as Meister Eckhart, Teresa of Avila, Angelus Silesius, and Jakob Böhme a support for this metaphor, for it is well known that these major figures sought in separation, solitude, and isolation the conditions to experience God directly and subjectively. In a gesture of opposition to *their* 'compact majority,' they attempted a spiritual experience that lay outside the traditional framework of theology. Mystical speech may be seen as a departure from the discourse of the group. In it, Lacan recognized the same trait Freud appreciated in a form of Judaism: a position in disagreement with the compact majority, with those idolaters for whom a golden calf covers the angst of loss and castration.

Chapter 5
Interpretation: Wandering and the Nomadism of the Letter

> *In each word many lights shine.*
>
> ZOHAR, iii, 202
>
> *Freud has developed on this basis an art of interpretation which takes on the task of, as it were, extracting the pure metal of the repressed thoughts from the ore of the unintentional ideas.*
>
> SIGMUND FREUD[1]

The relationship between the Jewish people and their God is structured around the Book of Books, particularly the Torah, or Revelation – a spoken and written code of communication between men and between man and God. This book and this tradition have functioned throughout the centuries both as the structuring axis of the religion, ethics, and politics of the Jewish people and as the space where Jews have developed a unique praxis of interpretation that has proved able to support the permanence of Judaism.

As nomadic as the Hebrew letters they find grouped over the white background of an ancient parchment, the doctors of the Law and commentators of the Text have always dared to say more than what was manifest in the Book, so that from time immemorial it has functioned as a territory that welcomes any number of emerging subjectivities. In their millennial wanderings, the Jewish people have used interpretation as a practice that allows the letters the possibility of being letters, using the white spaces in the Text as a reserve of meaning, always available to the reader/interpreter. This unceasing mission of reading the letters, multiplying their combinations, rewriting them in a continuous movement of unique signifying constructions concerning the origin, value, and meaning of life and death, eventually led to identifying the Jew as *he who knows how to read*. If it is true that religion begins where one stops reading,[2] it must be

---

[1] *SE*, vol. 7, p. 252. ["Freud's Psychoanalytic Procedure"]
[2] Winter, "Transmission et Talmude," *Bulletin interne de l'EFP*, vol II, juin 1979.

added that there is an atheism intrinsic to Judaism: it requires that the interpreter of Revelation desecrate it by causing it to be born again, re-creating it, inventing it as on the Day of Creation.

The Talmudist is par excellence a "traitor" to any unchanging "reading" – that is, any dogmatic reading – that blocks the production of thought. He asks himself what he reads and in this way elicits different meanings, never the same as before. As Henri Atlan has observed, this is a way of ensuring the enforcement of the anti-idolatrous second commandment. The struggle against idolatry avoids the illusion of possessing meaning. The Text is unconquerable and inapprehensible. In other words, "the paradoxes of language and its meaning are such that a discourse about God that is not idolatrous, that refrains from grasping or conquering his Name, is inevitably an atheistic discourse."[3]

Yet many Jews attempt to fill the unknown with words, investing the Sacred with a single meaning, a fixed sense. Those who give "a body" to the Text, a fixed image of it, elevate it to the category of an idol. Beyond the exegesis that proliferates within a given culture about which the exegete weaves commentaries that are immediately reabsorbed by tradition,[4] the Talmudic way of reading follows different paths: for linguistic and ethical reasons it is closer to the field of interpretation, in which the word coming from outside introduces a difference in the core of tradition. Indeed, the ways and methods of Jewish interpretation obey a unique, original style that requires the presence of an exteriority able to cause new words to be produced, beyond all knowledge of the Text. The reading of the Hebrew Bible, as David Banon observes, "is a permanent hemorrhage, by means of which the Text opens itself... showing forth the ethical order which underpins it."[5] Interpreters are unceasingly producing commentaries that go beyond any knowledge that has been converted into wis-

---

[3] Atlan, "Niveaux de signification et athéisme de l'écriture," in *La Bible au présent*, J. Halperin & G. Levitte (eds.), p. 86.

[4] In *L'Invention de la mythologie*, Marcel Detienne proposes, following the distinction anthropologists have made between exegesis and interpretation, the following formulations: exegesis is the unceasing commentary that a culture offers on its own symbolism, practices, and cultural repertoire as a whole. Exegetes produce discourses that have no other effect than to be reabsorbed by the commentary itself. Interpretation, however, is the result of an outside viewpoint that intervenes in the tradition of memory. If an interpretation is to become established, it must discuss, criticize, and transgress against tradition: the interpreter explodes a given meaning, to bring out the unspoken, other meanings.

[5] Banon, *La Lecture infinie*, p. 23.

dom. The scholarly Jewish reader of the Sacred Books does not decode them, nor does he limit himself to the available explanations. He is constantly returning to Scripture, creating, rewriting, and renewing, engaging in commerce with the Other and the world without appropriating the Other and the world. Talmudic reading is constantly going beyond the situation in which the texts were created, and in this sense it is always creative and transformative.

What is unique about the ancient Jewish scribes and interpreters of the Old Testament is that they made it impossible to give closure to these texts throughout the centuries. That is, they did not allow the letters of the scriptural text to become fixed, and thus opened the pages of the Bible to an infinite reading. The holy books of Judaism became an open work, since the rabbis and interpreters of Scripture have transformed these texts into a factory of other texts. In this way they have managed to preserve in the space of the Book the ever-visible subjectivity of the reader challenged by the riddle.

This is a kind of reading that allows each member of the community to differentiate himself or herself from all others, by formulating a commentary on the text the letters of which are gathered about a center empty of idols.[6] In addition, the work of transmitting and renewing Scripture testifies[7] to the transcendental character of meaning, always in movement, never grasped in a single signification. This is what makes it possible to establish surprising correspondences between deconstruction and other methods of reading proposed by contemporary linguistics, on the one hand, and the age-old method of interpretation of Jewish culture, on the other.[8]

We are now ready to discuss an old, vexed issue: the affinities between the way of interpreting the Biblical Text in Jewish culture and psychoanalytic interpretation. Karl Abraham was the first to call attention to a structural homology between these two kinds of interpretation. In his letter to Freud discussing the importance of having Jung as the head of the psychoanalytic movement, Abraham writes: "our Talmudic way of thinking cannot disappear just like that. Some days ago a small paragraph in *Jokes* [*and their Relation to the Unconscious*] strangely attracted me. When I looked

---

[6] As Gérard Pommier observes, in this sense the form of reading the Torah goes against racist ideology, since it ensures the subjectivity of each individual. Pommier, "À propos de l'anti-semitisme," p. 85.

[7] According to Banon's excellent studies in *La Lecture infinie, les voies de l'interprétation midrachique*.

[8] Ibid., p. 219.

at it more closely, I found that, in the technique of apposition and in its whole structure, it was completely Talmudic."[9]

It is well known that Freud always refused to subject his discovery to hermeneutic rationality, and that he was able to discover the key to dreams precisely because he was not a hermeneut himself.[10] When he established interpretation as one of the foundations of his clinical practice, Freud broke with the entire tradition of explanatory and descriptive hermeneutics, which did no more than reduce the subject to the condition of a mere object, capable of being interpreted by a predetermined code; instead, he resorted to the subject's speech.[11] This reversal of the relationship between knowledge and speech allowed the psychoanalytic method to give priority to the act of listening to and abandon the repetition of established meanings.

Freud underlined that the unconscious presented meanings and voices that testified to the overdetermination of its formations. At the same time, he was careful not to let psychoanalytic interpretation be reduced to a parasitic activity. In *The Interpretation of Dreams* he criticizes his colleague Wilhelm Stekel for attempting to reduce psychoanalytic interpretation to a purely exegetic endeavor, translating dream symbols instead of listening to the dreamer's associations.[12] Freud was opposed to a fixed gnosis of dreams symbols; he believed that interpretations were based upon the uniqueness of the subject's signifiers.

Psychoanalysis is not an exploratory or descriptive hermeneutics that reduces the subject to an object to be interpreted by the analyst. Nor is it a finished theory, a body of knowledge that can simply be applied in an exact, fixed, and unitary manner. This leads to a fundamental difference between the Freudian method and other psychotherapeutic practices. When Freud stopped using hypnosis and decided that the truth of the subject lay in the phenomenon of transference, he turned the entire thrust of interpretation away from any established body of knowledge.[13] By free-associating in the frame of the cure, the analysand produces the very knowledge she or he attributes to the analyst.

---

[9] Abraham to Freud, May 11, 1908 in H. Abraham and Ernst L. Freud (eds.), *A Psycho-analytic Dialogue*.

[10] See Michel Tort, "De l'interprétation ou la machine herméneutique."

[11] See Blanchot, *The Infinite Conversation*, Part II, Chapter 10.

[12] *SE*, vol. 5, p. 350. [*The Interpretation of Dreams*]

[13] Carlos Augusto Nicéas, "Respostas ao saber suposto," in Jorge Forbes (ed.), *Psicanálise ou psicoterapia*, p. 26.

Psychoanalytic interpretation pays attention to the unique function of the signifier in the analysand's speech, while encouraging a journey through different readings of one's own history. It allows the subject to reappropriate its own existence.

Unfolding of Meanings

The art of interpreting the sacred texts, developed within a particular experience, found support in what Lévinas calls the ethical principles of difference. The Text is a palimpsest and its signification is a becoming, distinct and transcendent.[14] In a Talmudic reading there is no conversion of the Other into the Same: interpretation takes place as an opening to the Unsayable. To read the Scriptures requires an intense effort in order to understand the word of a God who, after handing down His Law, remains silent.

It is written: "For [this law] is not a vain thing for you" (Deuteronomy 32:47). The Talmudists understood this Biblical verse in a quite literal sense: to them the holy word is filled with meanings, polysemic and multiple, open to the plurality of interpretations and meanings *to come*. The Text, like any work of art whose meaning is inexhaustible, is anchored in what lies beyond the symbolic; it is a texture of differences, creation *ex nihilo*. According to the Talmud, the Torah was handed to the people of Israel in a parchment of white fire and written in black fire. The white surrounding the black letters allowed the reading – since texts are made up not only of what is written but also of what is not written.[15]

The master commentators and the doctors of the Law turned Biblical narrative into a laboratory for new signification of the Text, a "migration" of letters, an exodus of words. This created a surplus of meaning,

---

[14] Lévinas writes: "The ethical order (re)conducts us toward God. A God who does not reveal Himself, for to do so would be to deny Himself, but who paradoxically preserves a relationship with the finite through the mark.... A God to whom one desires to have access, ever aware, however, that to go to Him is not to follow this mark, which is not a sign, but rather to go to the others who abide by this mark." Quoted in Banon, *op. cit.*, p. 255.

[15] In *Fragments of a Poetics of Fire* Bachelard observes that fire is restless and suggests intensity. In various cultures fire is considered one of the founding elements of civilization. In Greek myth, Prometheus stole the fire from the gods to give it to men, and for this he was subjected to unending torture. In the Hebrew myth of the writing of the Law, fire is also characterized as capable of changing and propagating itself.

which made it possible for the Book of Books to evolve into many other books,[16] which comprise the Oral Torah: the Targums, the Talmud, the Midrash, the Zohar and so on. Reading and interpreting became the sources of the art of writing, and Israel turned into a realm of writers: where the letter of God was, men's texts came to be. *Wo Es war, soll Ich werden.*[17]

The primary function of the Oral Law was to transmit the Scriptures to present and future generations. To the ancient Hebrews, the force of transmission lay in speech; this is why for centuries it was forbidden to transcribe the comments and interpretations of God's written word, preserved in the oral tradition. It was only in the second century of the Common Era, when the Jews were submitted to definitive dispersion and to ceaseless persecution that it became permissible to write down the Oral Torah; this resulted in the creation of such huge works as the Midrash and the Talmud. The dispersion of the Biblical text into other sacred writings coincided with the exile of the people of Israel.[18]

Etymologically, "Midrash" comes from the root *drash*, which means "demand," "search," "investigation." *Drash* is also one of the levels of meaning, the one concerned with seeking out what is not in the text. It is opposed to *pshat*, the literal sense of the text. In addition, there are two levels of meanings: *remez*, the allusive meaning, and *sod*, the secret meaning. The initials of these four terms form an acronym, *pardes*, meaning "orchard," "Paradise," or "garden of knowledge."

The Talmud presents us with an apologue on interpretation, enigmatically titled: "Do Not Interpret."

> According to our masters, four sages enter Paradise (Pardes): Ben Azzai, Ben Zoma, Ben Elisha (*Aher*) and Rabbi Akiba. Rabbi Akiba says: When you see pure marble stones, do not cry, Water! Water!, for it is said, 'He who speaks untruths shall not stand before My eyes' (Psalms 101:7). The first sage believes that what he sees is true; he dies. About him the Scriptures say, "Precious in the eyes of God is the death of His pious ones" (Psalms 116:15). The second gazes at the garden, and everything he sees seems double to him; he loses his sanity. Concerning him it is written: "Did

---

[16] Berenstein, "Um texto fora do lugar."

[17] *SE* vol. 22, p. 80 [*New Introductory Lectures on Psychoanalysis*, Lecture 31, "The Dissection of the Psychical Personality."].

[18] It should be kept in mind that the canon of Judaism does not consist of a single book: it is only the written Torah as clarified by the Talmud that inscribes the reader into the Jewish reading of the Scriptures. This is the meaning of the indissoluble bond between the written Torah and the Oral Torah.

you find honey? Eat only as much as you need, lest you be overfilled and vomit it up" (Proverbs 25:16). The third steps into the garden and begins to cut down the plantings. The world becomes strange; he abandons his faith and turns into someone else (*Aher*). The fourth, Rabbi Akiba, enters the garden and leaves it unharmed.[19]

    The story of the first sage relates to a meaning that is literally present in the text: *pshat*. The story of the second sage illustrates a meaning that is present, but incomplete: *remez*. The story of the third sage has to do with the deep meaning of the text: *drash*. The meaning is always absent, and the text demands a questioning, a going beyond. On this level of interpretation, a number of different readings coexist. Rabbi Ben Elisha, the third sage, becomes someone else (*Aher*). This rabbi, it is said, turned into a dissenter, a stranger, a heretic. Paradoxically, this apologue may suggest that the heretic attitude is the paradigm of Talmudic interpretation. The Midrash is a saying capable of going beyond what is known. On the fourth level, *sod*, the meaning is mysterious and secret. This is the remainder of the signifying operation of any interpretation. Every text leaves behind a mystery, as Rabbi Akiba realizes; he enters the paradise of language and emerges from it unscathed.

    The Talmud, which literally means "study," is the repository of transmission. *Lamed*, the only letter in the Hebrew alphabet that extends below the line, indicates a transgression and a search for interpretation beyond the text. What is transmitted is the way of commenting. The power of transmission lies in reading, in the manner of practicing such a reading, of producing ever-new words.

    The Talmud includes two sets of texts, one of them written in Hebrew (the Mishna) and the other in Aramaic (the Gemara). The Mishna, which etymologically means "repetition," is a treatise of civil and religious Jewish laws concerning six topics: the land, time, the feminine, society, the sacred, and death. Whereas the interpreters of the Midrash wrote comments that responded to the demand of interpretation posed by the very linguistic structure of the Sacred Text, the Talmud contains those texts that arose out of the people's need to adapt to new situations of life in successive generations. The interpreters of the Mishna attempted to find in the Hebrew Bible justification and groundings for the historical, geographic and cultural changes and adaptations of the Jewish people. While the Midrash presents oral law as an explanation of the Biblical text, in the

---

[19] Quoted in Banon, *La lecture infinie*, p. 204.

Talmud the transmission takes place independently of any explanatory order. One might say that the Midrash is an expression of the explanations and descriptions of the Biblical text, while the Talmudic interpretations go beyond the signs actually contained in the Torah and are expressions of the act of invention and creation of meaning. Biblical writing contains the past only to the extent that it is an organizing principle for the subject and the group. The Gemara – "completion," "addition" – is made out of commentaries on the Mishna. The interpreter goes from the Mishna to the Torah, never the other way around.

In *The Interpretation of Dreams,* Freud says that the dream must be dealt with as if it were Holy Scripture. Freud refers to the manifest content of the dream, fruit of a secondary elaboration, as the main text to study and deconstruct through free associations, since the primary elaboration of it is per se inaccessible. This trajectory echoes the articulation of the Mishna and the Gemara in the domain of The Holy Scriptures. The Talmud is equivalent to the language of dreams, the only one that can be spoken of, because what is written, the Torah, is lost.[20]

"You Are Requested to Close the Eyes": Reading-Writing

We may agree with Lévinas when he says that the interpretation of the Old Testament is part of Revelation. Hebrew is a language whose internal structure ensures a plurality of meanings; in fact, as Lacan pointed out, "the word is not a sign, but a net of significations."[21] The term that refers to the Hebrew language itself, Ivrit עברית has the same root עבר (*ayin-veth-resh*) as "transgression," "migration," and "rupture."

As is well known, Hebrew is a Semitic language with roots made up of three consonants, which admit multiple interpretations. The Hebrew alphabet, like the Arabic, contains only consonants, to which vowels are added for pronunciation, though usually not written. The fact that what is written cannot be pronounced and what is pronounced cannot be written gives Semitic languages an unfinished aspect: readers are constantly called upon to complete the text. Indeed, when dots representing vowels – *nekudot*, known as the souls of the letters – were added to the unpronounceable root, the ancient Hebrews re-created the meaning of writing each time they read. Little by little, the *matres lectionis* ("mothers of reading") were es-

---

[20] See Winter, "Transmission et Talmude," p. 194.
[21] Lacan, "Propos sur la causalité psychique," *Écrits*, p. 166.

tablished, that is, consonants that indicated the approximate value of the vocalic pronunciation (*aleph, he, waw, yod, heth* and *ayin*). Curiously enough, as several Talmudists have observed, three of these letters appear in the Tetragrammaton. The Greeks transcribed YHWH in their version of the Bible exclusively with vowels: Ιαουε.²²

In Hebrew, a given root may be actualized with vowels in a number of different ways, each of them with its own meaning, depending on the context and the interpreter. For instance, the three consonants of the Hebrew root s-p/f-r are associated with an indeterminate crossroads of meanings. The vowel points will indicate the sense given by the reader: *sefer* (book), *sofer* (writer), *sipur* (tale), *lesaper* (narrate), *sifrut* (literature), *sifriah* (library), and so on.²³ The consonantal structure of Hebrew, in which different vowels may be used with a single stable root, allows phonetic changes that bring about permanent changes in meaning. This is a language that ensures a space for the uniqueness of each subject's speech.

When souls are given to the letters, as the ancient scribes used to say, a word may yield absolutely uncanny meanings. The great twelfth-century French Talmudist Rashi renewed the Hebrew alphabet when he interpreted the passage from Exodus (3:14-5): "And God said unto Moses, I AM THAT I AM... this is my name for ever, and this is my memorial unto all generations." Referring to the Hebrew root of the word for "always" (*le'olam*) written without the *waw* (pronounced as "o") and pointing to the possibility that the root might incorporate another vowel, Rashi resorts to a teaching from the Talmud and interprets God's answer as meaning: "My name must remain hidden." Now, "hidden" in Hebrew is *'alum*, and it has the same root (*'ayin-lamed-mem*) as *le'olam*, "always" or "forever."²⁴ Homography (words written with the same root) and heterophony (each root read differently) are the mark of the experience of language that is to be found on the pages of the Talmud.

Hebrew allows for the existence of opposites and contradictions within a given statement: the root of the word "repeat" (*lishnot*) is the same as that of "change" (*leshanot*): *shin, nun, teth*. This is reminiscent of one of the paradigms that Freud discovered for reading dream language: "The way in

---

²² In *Naissance et renaissance de l'écriture*, p. 129, Gérard Pommier observes: "if all the letters in the Tetragrammaton have turned into vowels in Greek and if every consonant requires a vowel to be read, then the name of a vocalic god will be present every time one pronounces a consonant, in itself unpronounceable without a variable vocalic breath."

²³ The example is taken from Banon, *La lecture infinie*, p. 194.

²⁴ Ibid., p. 28.

which dreams treat the category of contraries and contradictories is highly remarkable. It is simply disregarded."[25]

The relationship between the Holy Books and Jewish people establishes a unique, original form of reading that "attempts to set free, beyond the signs actually written, the 'fullness of meanings' of meaning."[26] Reading the Text is a form of transformation and creation. It is a task similar to what Freud attributes to the "dream-work."

You are requested to close the eyes. This sentence appeared in a dream Freud had after his father's funeral.[27] He wrote to Fliess that his dream sentence was associated with the fact that he had gone to a barbershop on the day of his father's funeral; this is why he arrived late at the funeral and added to the frustration of his family, who resented his decision to give his father a quiet and simple burial.[28] In *Traumdeutung* Freud represents his dream in the following manner:

>   the
> You are requested to close   eye(s).
>   an

"Each of these two versions had a meaning of its own and led in a different direction when the dream was interpreted," Freud writes.[29] The inscription "You are requested to close an eye" begs his family's indulgence for his arriving late for the funeral. On the other hand, "You are requested to close the eyes" represents one's sacred duty toward the dead, and one which Freud performed for his father: "I had chosen the simplest possible ritual for the funeral, for I knew my father's own views on such ceremonies."[30]

---

[25] *SE*, vol. 11, p. 153 ["The Antithetical Meaning of Primal Words"]. In Semitic grammar, as Botero remarks in *The Birth of God*, there is no equivalent to the subordinate clause, so that clauses are nearly always coordinated using "and… and… and" instead of "since," "in order to," "when" or even the alternative conjunction *or*. The relational logic of a language where the verb *to be* is replaced by conjunctions implies a reality of constant interactions. See also Deleuze, *The Logic of Sense*.

[26] Banon, *La lecture infinie*, p. 17.

[27] Freud describes *The Interpretation of Dreams* as "a portion of my own self-analysis, my reaction to my father's death — that is to say, to the most important event, the most poignant loss, of a man's life." *SE*, vol. 4, p. xxvi.

[28] In his letter to Fliess of Nov. 2, 1896 Freud writes: "One should do one's duty toward the dead in two senses: (a) apology, as if I hadn't done my duty and my conduct needed to be overlooked; (b) the duty in the literal sense." *The Letters of Sigmund Freud*.

[29] *SE*, vol. 4, p. 318. [*The Interpretation of Dreams*]

[30] Ibid.

A variety of meanings, whether in psychoanalytic or in Talmudic interpretation, does not mean that any meaning is possible. A reading is not arbitrary, because each reader's subjectivity is engraved by the Jewish historical context leading to an unfolding of meanings. Truth is *nomadic*; the Text is atopic. "The book of wandering is no more than the wandering of the book,"[31] writes Jabès. Soon the reader is left landless – he cannot settle anywhere – and nomadism means not to own anything.[32]

If the Hebrew language by itself requires interpretation, so does the manner in which the Biblical text is written since it does not contain punctuation but is an almost uninterrupted sequence of signs. Every now and then a few conjunctive-disjunctive accents have the function of establishing a rhythm in order to produce meaning, as in the case of *te'amim* – a word derived from *ta'am*, which means "to taste," "to discriminate." These accents allow pause and modulation, indicating that there is association or dissociation between letters. According to some students and commentators of the Sacred Text, the Torah is a single long sentence, transcribed on a roll of parchment, a sentence that can be read as the parchment is unrolled.

From a methodological viewpoint, the first thing that interpreters had to do was to introduce breaks between letters in order to create words and spaces between them for sentences to appear. It was then possible for the rabbis to give various interpretations; each blank space introduced by the interpreter's break became "a reserve of meaning available to the reader."[33] As Barthes points out in *The Pleasure of the Text*, writers and readers are submitted to the primacy of the letter, a primacy that dissipates any fixed signification.

Lévinas recalls that his Talmud master had 120 different interpretations for this verse in the Pentateuch: "Speak unto the children of Israel, *le'emor*, in these terms." Another interpretation separates the *aleph* (which sounds like "eh") and write *l'o'emor*, "not to say," so that the Talmudist read the verse as follows: "Speak unto the children of Israel, telling them not to say" – which takes the meaning: "It is necessary not to say so that the listener may begin to think." Lévinas's reading of the same Biblical passage phoneticized the root of the word *le'emor* ("to say") differently: "Speak unto the children of Israel, telling them to say" – i.e.: "Teach the children of Israel so deeply that they will understand to the point of saying."[34]

---

[31] Jabès, quoted in Ouaknin, *Le Livre brûlé: Lire le Talmude*, p. 59.
[32] Blanchot, *The Infinite Conversation*, p. 125.
[33] Banon, *La lecture infinie*, p. 210.
[34] The example is taken from Ouaknin, *Le Livre brûlé: Lire le Talmude*, p. 28.

Signs do not point to a fixed meaning, but to a diversity of senses. It is also important to underscore the fact that all interpretations coexist on the page of the Talmud, even when they are mutually contradictory. This unique trait of preserving the contradictions in the very heart of tradition characterizes a certain kind of Judaism, developed in the passion for the letter, as an anti-dogmatic doctrine committed to the plurality of meanings and the production of thought. For it is written: "Two opinions are words of God."[35]

In psychoanalysis the same dream may give rise to a certain interpretation at the beginning of the treatment and, years later, to a different one. As *Die Traumdeutung* states, "It is only with the greatest difficulty that the beginner in the business of interpreting dreams can be persuaded that his task is not at an end when he has a complete interpretation in his hands – an interpretation which makes sense, is coherent and throws light upon every element of the dream's content. For the same dream may perhaps have another interpretation as well, an 'over-interpretation', which has escaped him."[36] The analytic method uses cuts and anagrams to bring to light what had been repressed.[37] Freud compares the activity of the analyst to that of the chemist, in that if psychoanalysis implies separating, cutting, and dividing mental processes into elementary components, it does not imply syntheses.[38]

Memory and Time: To Repeat the Future

The endless reading of the Torah goes beyond the mere assurance of memory against the erosion of time; it is the very movement of transmission: "Neither with you only do I make this covenant and this oath; but with him that standeth here with us this day before the Lord our God, and also with him that is not here with us this day" (Deut. 29:14-5).

The narrative of Genesis shows that what is essential in it is not what happened in the beginning, but the fact that there is a beginning. Creation

---

[35] Bavli Talmud, quoted in Banon, *La lecture infinie*, p. 68.

[36] *SE*, vol. 4, p. 523. [*The Interpretation of Dreams*]

[37] To mention one example among many, in *Notes on a Case of Obsessional Neurosis* Freud breaks down the Rat Man's magical formula *Gleijisamen*, into *Gisela* and *Samen* (semen). *SE*, vol. 10, pp. 281-82.

[38] *SE*, vol. 17, p. 159. ["Lines of Advance in Psycho-Analytic Therapy"]

is manifested by the appearance of a time.[39] Something has a beginning *sine die*, since it is absolute creation, without end, past, or present, pure becoming. In this framework, the Covenant should be understood as an ineradicable link between Jewishness and the future; Jewishness is *being-open-to-the-future*, that is, the ability "to hold one's identity, reflect it, declare it, announce it to oneself, only out of what comes from the future to come."[40] Jewishness is founded "after the event, retroactively: I assume today what in the absolute past of the origin had no subject to receive it."[41]

In psychoanalysis as well, history associates past and present. The past coexists with the present.[42] Both psychoanalysis and Judaism treat the past-present relationship differently than the usual approach in the West, where historiography places them side by side, never both *at the same time*. In Western historiography past and present are associated in the modes of "succession (one after the other), correlation (greater or lesser proximity), effect (one is caused by the other), or disjunction (either one or the other, never the two together)."[43] The interpreter of Talmud is ethically required not to be temporally distanced from it. In each age, in each generation, the reader must interpret subjectively what is transmitted to him or her, preserving the traditional structures of transmission and ensuring their continuity. The interpreter cannot simply move back to a past time, but must actively participate in the transmission by producing multiple new meanings for the letter of the Text.[44]

Under the Biblical imperative of *Zakhor, Israel!* the Jewish people is urged to remember. This commandment has had an enduring effect on Jews since Biblical times. *Zakhor*, which means "to remember," indicates the Jewish understanding of history as a logical knot between present and past.

---

[39] André Neher, "Vision du temps et de l'histoire dans la culture juive," in Ricœur, *Les Cultures et le temps*, pp. 171-92.

[40] Derrida, *Archive Fever*, p. 74.

[41] Lévinas, *Totality and Infinity*, p. 56.

[42] The notion of virtuality often appears in contemporary philosophy, in various authors. It refers to a form of reality to be distinguished from bodily or material reality. "Perhaps the term virtuality means exactly the mode of the structure or the object of theory as long as we subtract from it all its vagueness; for the virtual has a reality of its own, but one not to be mistaken for any actual reality, any present or past actuality; it has an ideality that is characteristic of it but should not be mistaken for any possible image, any abstract idea." Deleuze, "A quoi reconnaît-on le structuralisme?" in Châtelet, *Histoire de la Philosophie, idées, doctrines*, vol. 8, p. 283.

[43] de Certeau, *Histoire et psychanalyse entre science et fiction*, p. 99.

[44] See Ouaknin, *Le Livre brûlé: Lire le Talmude*, p. 12.

If the command to remember is absolute, there is, nonetheless, an almost desperate pathos about the Biblical concern with memory, and a shrewd wisdom that knows how short and fickle human memory can be. Not history, as is commonly supposed, but only mythic time repeats itself. If history is real, then the Red Sea can be crossed only once, and Israel cannot stand twice at Sinai, a Hebrew counterpart, if you wish, to the wisdom of Heraclitus. Yet the Covenant is to endure forever. "I make this covenant, with its sanctions, not with you alone, but both with those who are standing here with us this day before the Lord our God, and also with those who are not with us here this day" (Deut. 29:13-14). It is an outrageous claim. Surely there will be a day "when your children will ask you in time to come, saying: What mean you by these stones? Then you shall say to them: Because the waters of the Jordan were cut off before the ark of the covenant of the Lord when it passed through the Jordan" (Josh. 4:6-7). Not the stone, but the memory transmitted by the fathers, is decisive if the memory embedded in the stone is to be conjured out of it to live again for subsequent generations. If there can be no return to Sinai, then what took place at Sinai must be borne along the conduits of memory to those who were not there that day.[45]

The Jewish tradition of remembering does not consist only in preserving a heritage. *Zakhor* means turning memory into an adventure of creative historicity on the basis of a set of traits that must be permanently reinscribed, in each generation, by all subjects, but always individually and differentially. Perception of history in Judaism does not obey linear temporality. In each era, in each generation, the reader interprets subjectively what is transmitted to him or her, preserving the tradition of transmission and ensuring its continuity.

It might then be said that historical consciousness has become "the effect of a multiplicity of voices in which echoes of the past are heard,"[46] which paradoxically are also echoes of the future. Memory is not a past that needs to be understood, but a presence that returns in order to "repeat a path that has never been followed."[47]

This is most evident in the Haggada,[48] where the logic of a time that

---

[45] Yerushalmi, *Zakhor*, p. 10.
[46] Banon, *La lecture infinie*, p. 176.
[47] Quoted in Ouaknin, *Le Livre brûlé: Lire le Talmude*, p. 54.
[48] Talmudic literature that contains not only explanations and interpretations of and comments on Biblical stories but also legends, narratives about post-Biblical everyday Jewish life, as well as anecdote and philosophical, scientific, and ethical discussions.

cannot be measured by the clock or the calendar underlies a unique process of historicity; the transmission from one generation to another is a search, a questioning (*drash*) about the meanings of a text written in the desert and fertilized a posteriori by the breath (*ruach*) of the mute letters of the Hebrew language. The rabbis and Hebrew scholars make present and past coexist in a tireless struggle to interpret the history of the Jewish people in terms of their own generation and subsequent generations. If in the Bible time follows a chronological order, in the world of the Haggada interpretations generate a different time: Adam teaches the Torah to his son, and Moses frequents a synagogue in the Middle Ages.[49] One may say that Talmudic temporality engenders difference, the new, so that the traces of memory are transmitted meaningfully on the basis of the relations between past and present. Moses crosses the desert in Biblical antiquity and in the Middle Ages as well as in modern times, and will go on doing so as many times as it is necessary for him to cross the desert, probably forever. The alterity expressed by the Text ensures the permanent exodus of the letters, which is repeated for every generation and for every subject.

In his reflections concerning history and psychoanalysis, de Certeau observes that "psychoanalysis is articulated on the process that is the very core of Freud's discovery: the return of the repressed."[50] He notes that this mechanism is a sign of the past time that inhabits the present as virtuality. Indeed, in Freud, clinical experiences show past and present intertwined.

> As you know, I am working on the assumption that our psychic mechanism has come into being by a process of stratification: the material present in the form of memory traces being subjected from time to time to a *rearrangement* in accordance with fresh circumstances – to a *retranscription*. Thus what is essentially new about my theory is the thesis that memory is present not once but several times over, that it is laid down in various kinds of indications.... I should like to emphasize the fact that the successive registrations represent the psychic achievement of successive epochs of life. At the boundary between two such epochs a translation of the psychic material must take place.[51]

According to Freud, history cannot be reduced to a mere temporal succession: always elaborated in the present, it contains a retranscription

---

[49] Yerushalmi, *Zakhor*, p. 17.
[50] de Certau, *Histoire et psychanalyse*, p. 97.
[51] Freud to Fliess, Letter 52, Dec. 6, 1896, in *Freud/Fliess*, ed. Masson, pp. 207-13.

of the past that updates it and invests it with new meaning. By means of permanent retranscriptions historical truth is transmitted from one generation to another.[52]

Clinical analysis goes in a direction opposite to that of historiography, developing a logic "familiar to the Semitic and Jewish historical tradition of formal stories, of language games."[53] Jean-Pierre Winter remarks that the anti-idolatrous position of the readers of the Book has ensured the transmission of Judaism throughout the centuries. This tradition of interpretation, separation, appropriation, exile, and production of difference is shared by psychoanalysis and grounds the transmission of Freud's discovery.

In implying a living experience that cannot be reduced to any presupposed interpretation or knowledge, Jewish reading causes each subject to remember the ineradicable trace of the Covenant and announces it to the future. In psychoanalysis, interpretation is the instrument that gives a voice to what once worked in silence, toward a difference that is to come, punctually and evanescently. Both instances turn upon the power of a singular word, experienced as unique.

---

[52] It should be stressed that the question of time, memory, and history accompanies the entirety of Freud's work. It marks the discovery of psychoanalysis as a differential technique from hypnosis; it becomes the essential element of the theory of seduction first and of its dismantling later, with the acknowledgment of the role played by phantasies in psychic life; it defines the timing of psychic causality (*nachträglich*), the significance of screen memories, the particularity of repetition in the transference; it informs the modalities of interpretations and the use of constructions in the cure.

[53] de Certeau, *op. cit.*, p. 128.

Conclusion

> *In stating what has been said, one has to restate what has never been said.*
>
> MICHEL FOUCAULT [1]

If Jewishness is a construction, a becoming, Freud's "becoming-Jew" goes with his discovery of psychoanalysis. In his refusal of a Jewish religious identity, in his never-ending search for the nonidentical, in his own exoduses, Freud's invention of Jewishness corresponds with the construction of psychoanalysis as a practice and a theory. Far from supporting normative identifications, psychoanalysis helps the subject to find in the rigor of the word his or her uniqueness, style, and absolute difference.

From this point of view, *Der Mann Moses und die monotheistische Religion* establishes a fundamental link between Jewishness and psychoanalysis. In 1934, as the Nazis burned many of his books and writings in Berlin bonfires, Freud, refusing to be intimidated by such a barbarity, began to write his "historical novel." If they burned his books, what he could still do was to gather the letters from the fire and write other books. Freud went on writing, unintimidated by the climate of fear and horror that preceded the extermination.

Throughout his work, Freud took pains not to allow psychoanalysis to become identical to itself. With his *Der Mann Moses und die monotheistische Religion* he opens new ways for transmitting the experienced-non-experienced, the familiar-foreign, the known-unknown. When he was forced to flee Austria, Freud suggested to the Executive Committee of the Vienna Psychoanalytic Society to act like the ancient Jews when the Temple of Jerusalem was destroyed: "After the destruction of the Temple... Rabbi Jochanan bem Sakkai asked for permission to open a school at Jabneh for the study of the Torah. We are going to do the same. We are, after all, used to persecution by our history, tradition, and some of us by personal experience." [2]

---

[1] Foucault, *The Birth of the Clinic*, p. xviii.
[2] Quoted in Jones, *Life and Works*, vol. 3, p. 221. Freud left four sisters in Vienna. At first

Endurance and determination in transmitting newborn psychoanalysis was Freud's response to obstacles and persecution until the end. Yet Freud could foresee how many psychoanalysts driven into exile would not be able to survive without creating golden calves for their own use. Sadly he anticipated how some of them would deviate from the true object of psychoanalysis. "Sometimes I am amazed that analysts themselves should not be radically changed by their relation with analysis."[3]

The history of the discovery of psychoanalysis and the history of its institutions are interconnected, although the former should be distinguished from the latter, as Freud himself pointed out.[4] From its very beginnings, the process of institutionalization of psychoanalysis generated a discrepancy between the goals of the movement and its use. Political conformism was supported to the detriment of research and knowledge. The external threat to which psychoanalysis was subjected at its inception was now substituted by the corrosive nature of stereotypical institutionalization. The experience of exile structural to the analytic process was undermined by the forced identification with an *esprit de corps*.

The practice of reading and researching, of applying clinical discoveries to an enlargement of theory, was largely substituted by the adherence to a rigid dogma or to the protocol of accepted and acceptable knowledge, established by institutional corporation. The emphasis shifted from research to professionalization, to the attempt to create a monopoly over training, in order to protect specific interests. This led to the establishment of stereotypical programs, which favored stereotypical writings and the repetition of the dominant discourse. The very core of Freud's discovery – psychoanalysis as a practice of uniqueness and difference – was substituted for a repertoire of *idées fixes* of a theocratic nature.

---

they were all confined to a single room of the family apartment. Marie, Adolfine and Pauline were sent to Theresienstadt. Adolphine died, according to the official record, from "internal hemorrhage"; Marie and Pauline were sent to the extermination camp of Maly Trostinec; and Rosa went to Treblinka. At the Nuremberg trials it was revealed that Rosa, as soon as she arrived at the extermination camp, was sent to the gas chamber immediately after presenting herself to the commander of the German army as one of Sigmund Freud's sisters. See Fuks, "Das armas e dos deuses," pp. 118-9.

[3] Freud, letter to Laforgue, Feb. 5, 1928, in André Bourguignon, *O conceito de renegação em Freud*, p. 27.

[4] *SE*, vol. 14, p. 16. ["On The History of the Psycho-Analytic Movement"]

"The atheist as fighter and as revolutionary is not the one who denies God... but the one who asserts himself as one serving no god."[5] Many analysts have given up Freudian ethics, becoming the enemies of the discourse they are supposed to transmit.

Could it be that psychoanalysis is a cause inevitably fated to fail in its own institution? This is a question every analyst should address in order never to cease to support transmission and identify its resistances, even when they arise from the very place that should protect psychoanalysis. It is imperative to distinguish between authentic psychoanalytic discourse and its perverse popularization.

"Never say you have arrived; for everywhere you are a passenger in transit."[6]

---

[5] Lacan, *L'Angoisse*, p. 358.
[6] Jabès quoted in Ouaknin, *Le Livre brulé*, p. 279.

Bibliography

Abraham, Hilda C., & Ernst L. Freud (eds.). *A Psycho-analytic Dialogue: The Letters of Sigmund Freud and Karl Abraham 1907-1926*. Trans. Bernard Marsh & Hilda C. Abraham. London: The Hogarth Press, 1965.
Anzieu, Didier. *Freud's Self-Analysis*. Guilford, CT: International Universities Press, 1986.
Appiah, Kwame Anthony. *In My Father's House: Africa in the Philosophy of Culture*. Oxford: Oxford University Press, 1993.
Arendt, Hannah. *The Jew as Pariah: Jewish Identity and Politics in the Modern Age*. New York: Grove Press, 1978.
_____ *The Origins of Totalitarianism*. New York: Harcourt Brace & Company, 1979.
_____ *Rahel Varnhagen: The Life of a Jewess*. Baltimore: Johns Hopkins University Press, 1997.
Armstrong, Karen. *A History of God: The 4000-Year Quest of Judaism, Christianity and Islam*. New York: Ballantine Books, 1994.
Assoun, Paul-Laurent. *Le Freudisme*. Paris: PUF, 2001.
_____ "Le Sujet et l'Autre chez Lévinas et Lacan." *Rue Descartes* 7 *(Logiques de l'éthique)*. Paris: Albin Michel, juin. 1993.
_____ *La Métapsychologie*. Paris: PUF, 1993.
_____ "El sujeto del Ideal", *Malestar en la cultura*. Buenos Aires: Manantial, 1987.
Atlan, Henri. "Niveaux de signification et athéisme de l'écriture." In J. Halperin & G. Levitte (eds.), *La Bible au présent*. Idées/Gallimard, 1982.
Bachelard, Gaston et al. *Fragments of a Poetics of Fire*. Dallas: Dallas Institute Publications, 1991.
Badiou, Alain. *Ethics: An Essay on the Understanding of Evil*. London: Verso Books, 2001.
Bakan, David. *Sigmund Freud and the Jewish Mystical Tradition*. Princeton: D. Van Nostrand, 1958.
Balmé, François, et al. *Freud et Moïse: Écritures du Père*. Paris: Éres, 1997.
Banon, David. *La Lecture infinie, les voies de l'interprétation midrachique*. Paris: Seuil, 1987.
_____ "L'Appel de l'autre." *L'Arche*, no. 459 (*Lévinas, philosophe et juif*). Paris: 1995.
Barnard, Suzanne, & Bruce Fink (eds). *Reading Seminar XX*. State Univ of New York Press, 2002.
Barthes, Roland. *Mythologies*. London: Jonathan Cape, 1972.
_____ *The Pleasure of the Text*. New York: Farrar, Straus and Giroux, 1975.
Beller, Steven. *Vienna and the Jews, 1867-1938: A Cultural History*. Cambridge: Cambridge University Press, 1991.
Berenstein, Lena. "Um texto fora do lugar." *Trieb. Revista da Sociedade Brasileira de Psicanálise do Rio de Janeiro* 1, 1995, p. 3.
Bergman, Martin S. "Moses and the Evolution of Freud's Identity." In Martimer Ostow (ed.), *Judaism and Psychoanalysis*. New York: Ktav, 1982.
Birman, Joel. *Psicanálise, ciência e cultura*. Rio de Janeiro: Jorge Zahar Editor, 1994.
_____ *Freud e a interpretação psicanalítica*. Rio de Janeiro: Relume Dumará, 1991.

Bibliography

_____ *Ensaios de teoria psicanalítica*. Rio de Janeiro: Jorge Zahar Editor, 1993.
Blanchot, Maurice. *The Infinite Conversation*. Minneapolis: University of Minnesota Press, 1992.
Bloom, Harold. *Ruin the Sacred Truths: Poetry and Belief from the Bible to the Present*. Cambridge, MA: Harvard University Press, 1991.
Borges, Jorge Luis. *A History of Eternity*. In J. L. Borges, *Nonfictions*, New York: Viking, 1999/2000.
Borges, Njaine Sherrine. *Metamorfoses do corpo: uma pedagogia freudiana*. Rio de Janeiro, Fiocruz, 1996.
Bottero, Jean. *The Birth of God: The Bible and the Historian*. University Park, PA: Pennsylvania State University Press, 2000.
Bourguignon, André. *O conceito de renegação em Freud*. Rio de Janeiro: Jorge Zahar Editor, 1991.
Boyarin, Daniel. *Carnal Israel: Reading Sex in Talmudic Culture*. Berkeley: University of California Press, 1995.
_____ "This we know to be the carnal Israel." Chicago: *Critical Inquiry*, 18, pp. 474-505.
Brunel, Pierre (ed.). *Companion to Literary Myths, Heroes and Archetypes*. London: Routledge, 1995.
Buci-Glucksmann, Christine. "Figures viennoises de l'alterité. Feminité et judaïté." In Marie Moscovici & Jean-Michel Rey (eds.), *L'Écrit du temps*. Paris: Minuit, 1984.
Campos, Haroldo de (trans. and ed.). *Eclesiastes. Poema sapiencial. Qohélet / o-que-se-sabe*. São Paulo: Perspectiva, 1990.
Cassirer, Ernst. *Language and Myth*. New York: Dover, 1946.
_____ *Mythical Thought*. Vol. 2 of *The Philosophy of Symbolic Forms*. New Haven: Yale University Press, 1971.
Châtelet, François (ed.). *Histoire de la Philosophie, idées, doctrines*. Paris: Hachette, 1972-3.
Chemama, Roland, & Bernard Vandermersch (eds.). *Dictionnaire de la Psychanalyse*. Paris: Larousse, 2003.
Chemouni, Jacques. *Freud et le sionisme*. Paris: Solin, 1988.
Chnaiderman, Mirian. "Derrida em Freud: a tradução impossível, o desvario necessário." In Célio Garcia et al., *Tempo Brasileiro*, no. 70 *(Em torno de Freud)*. Rio de Janeiro, 1982.
Chourraki, André. "Traduire la Bible." In Marie Moscovici & Jean-Michel Rey (eds.), *L'Écrit du temps*. Paris: Minuit, 1984.
Coutinho Jorge, Marco Antonio. *Sexo e discurso em Freud e Lacan*. Rio de Janeiro: Jorge Zahar Editor, 1988.
de Certeau, Michel. *Histoire et psychanalyse entre science et fiction*. Paris: Gallimard, Paris, 1987.
_____ *The Writing of History*. New York: Columbia University Press, 1992.
Defontaine, Jeanne. "Expérience culturelle et perte du sens: dè-significations et malaise d'une indifférence." *Revue Française de Psychanalyse*, vol. 57. Paris: 1993.
Deleuze, Gilles. *The Logic of Sense*. New York: Columbia University Press, 1990.
_____ "A quoi reconnaît-on le structuralisme?" In François Châtelet (ed.), *Histoire de la philosophie*. Paris : Hachette, 1973.
_____ & Felix Guattari. *What is Philosophy?* New York: Columbia University Press, 1996.
_____ *A Thousand Plateaus: Capitalism and Schizophrenia*. London: Athlone, 1988.
Derrida, Jacques. *Writing and Difference*. Chicago: University of Chicago Press, 1978.
_____ *Archive Fever: A Freudian Impression*. Chicago: University of Chicago Press, 1997.

_____ "Adieu." *L'Arche*, no. 459 (*Lévinas, philosophe et juif*). Paris: 1995.
Detienne, Marcel. *L'invention de la mythologie*. Paris: Gallimard, 1991.
Deutscher, Isaac. *The Non-Jewish Jew and Other Essays*. Oxford: Oxford University Press, 1968.
Ducrot, O. & Todorov, T. *Dictionnaire encyclopédique des sciences du langage*. Paris : Éditions du Seuil, 1972.
Eco, Umberto. *The Open Work*. Cambridge, MA: Harvard University Press, 1989.
Eliade, Mircea. *Myth and Reality*. New York: HarperCollins, 1968.
Enriquez, Eugène. "Un peuple immortel?" In Marie Moscovici & Jean-Michel Rey (eds.), *L'Écrit du temps*. Paris: Minuit, 1984.
Falzeder, Ernst, et al. (eds.). *The Complete Correspondence of Sigmund Freud and Karl Abraham, 1907-1925*. Cambridge, MA: Harvard University Press, 1996.
Figueiredo, Luiz Cláudio. "O interesse de Lévinas para a psicanálise: desinteresse do rosto." *Caderno de Subjetividade* I/1, 1993, pp. 39-51.
Flem, Lydia. *Freud et ses patients*. Paris: Le Livre de Poche, 1993.
_____ *Freud the Man: An Intellectual Biography*. New York: The Other Press, 2003.
Forbes, Jorge (ed.). "Uma questão de sobrevivência: notas sobre Freud e a IPA." In Jorge Forbes (org.), *A escola de Lacan: a formação do psicanalista e a transmissão da psicanálise*. Campinas: Papirus, 1984.
_____ *Psicanálise ou psicoterapia*. Campinas: Papirus, 1997.
Foucault, Michel. *The Order of Things: An Archaeology of Human Sciences*. New York: Vintage Books 1994.
_____ "What Is an Author?" In Vassilis Lambropoulos and David Neal Miller (eds), *Twentieth-Century Literary Theory*. Albany: State University Press of New York, 1987.
Freud, Sigmund. *The Origins of Psycho-Analysis: Letters to Wilhelm Fliess, Drafts and Notes: 1887-1902*. Marie Bonaparte, Anna Freud, & Ernst Kris (eds.). New York: Basic Books, and London: Imago Publishing Company, 1954.
_____ *Standard Edition of the Complete Psychological Works (SE)*. Trans. and ed. by James Strachey. London: Hogarth Press, 1975.
_____ "The Psychotherapy of Hysteria" (1885). *SE*, vol. 2.
_____ "Screen Memories" (1899). *SE*, vol. 3.
_____ *The Interpretation of Dreams* (1900). *SE*, vols. 4 and 5.
_____ "On Psychotherapy" (1905). *SE*, vol. 7.
_____ *Jokes and their Relation to the Unconscious* (1905). *SE*, vol. 8.
_____ *Delusions and Dreams in Jensen's "Gradiva"* (1907). *SE*, vol. 9.
_____ "Analysis of a Phobia in a Five-Year-Old Boy" (1909). *SE*, vol. 10.
_____ "Notes upon a Case of Obsessional Neurosis" (1909). *SE*, vol. 10.
_____ "The Antithetical Meaning of Primal Words" (1910). *SE*, vol. 11.
_____ "The Significance of Sequences of Vowels" (1911). *SE*, vol. 12.
_____ "The Dynamics of Transference" (1912). *SE*, vol. 12.
_____ *Totem and Taboo* (1912). *SE*, vol. 13.
_____ "On The History of the Psycho-Analytic Movement" (1914). *SE*, vol. 14.
_____ "Remembering, Repeating, Working-Through" (1914). *SE*, vol. 12.
_____ "Observations on Transference-Love" (1915). *SE*, vol. 15.
_____ "On Transience" (1916). *SE*, vol. 14.
_____ *Introductory Lectures on Psycho-Analysis* (1916). *SE*, vol. 15.
_____ "A Difficulty in the Path of Psycho-Analysis" (1917). *SE*, vol. 17.
_____ "Lines of Advance in Psycho-Analytic Therapy" (1919). *SE*, vol. 17.
_____ "The 'Uncanny'" (1919). *SE*, vol. 17.
_____ *Beyond the Pleasure Principle* (1920). *SE*, vol. 18.

Bibliography

_____ *Group Psychology and the Analysis of the Ego* (1921). *SE*, vol. 18.
_____ "Two Encyclopaedia Articles" (1923). *SE*, vol. 18.
_____ *The Ego and the Id* (1923). *SE*, vol. 10.
_____ "An Autobiographical Study" (1925). *SE*, vol. 20.
_____ "The Resistances to Psycho-Analysis" (1925). *SE*, vol. 19.
_____ "Address to the Society of B'nai B'rith" (1941). *SE*, vol. 20.
_____ "The Question of Lay Analysis" (1926). *SE*, vol. 20.
_____ *The Future of an Illusion* (1927). *SE*, vol. 21.
_____ *Civilization and Its Discontents* (1930). *SE*, vol. 21.
_____ *New Introductory Lectures on Psycho-Analysis* (1932). *SE*, vol. 22.
_____ "Femininity" (1933). *SE*, vol. 22.
_____ "Why war?" (1933). *SE*, vol. 22.
_____ "A Disturbance of Memory on the Acropolis" (1936). *SE*, vol. 22.
_____ "Constructions in Analysis" (1937). *SE*, vol. 23.
_____ *Moses and Monotheism* (1939). *SE*, vol. 23.
_____ "Death and Us." In Ostow, Mortimer (ed.), *Judaism and Psychoanalysis*; New York: Ktav, 1982.
_____ *The Complete Letters of Sigmund Freud to Wilhelm Fliess 1887-1904*. Trans. and ed. by Jeffrey Moussaieff Masson. Cambridge, MA and London: Belknap Press, Harvard University Press, 1985.
_____. "O valor da vida." 1926 interview with George S. Viereck. In Souza, Paulo César de (ed.). *O gabinete do dr. Lacan*. São Paulo: Brasiliense, 1990.
_____ *The Letters of Sigmund Freud to Eduard Silberstein, 1871-1881*, Cambridge, MA: Harvard University Press, 1991.
_____ *The Letters of Sigmund Freud*. Ed. by Ernst L. Freud. New York: Dover, 1992.
_____ & Pfister, O. *Psychoanalysis and faith: The Letters of Sigmund Freud and Oskar Pfister*. New York: Basic Books, 1963.
_____ & Zweig, Arnold. *The Letters of Sigmund Freud and Arnold Zweig*. Ed. by Ernst L. Freud. New York: NYU Press, 1987.
_____ *The Diary of Sigmund Freud - 1929/1939: a chronicle of events in the last decade*. London: Freud Museum Publications, 1992.
Fuks, B., Betty. "Uma ferida narcísica." Marcos Comaru & Maria Carmem Maya (eds.), *Neurose obsessiva*. Rio de Janeiro: Letter, 1992.
_____ "Das armas e dos deuses." *Tempo Psicanalítico: Angústia*. Rio de Janeiro: SPID, 1994.
_____ "As escrituras e o Talmude: a singularidade de uma hermenêutica." *Agalma*, Escola Brasileira de Psicanálise do Campo Freudiano, 2 (7). Bahia, Mar. 1976.
Garcia-Roza, Luiz Alfredo. *O mal radical em Freud*. Rio de Janeiro: Jorge Zahar, 1990.
Gay, Peter. *Freud: A Life for Our Time*. London: Dent, 1988.
_____ *A Godless Jew: Freud, Atheism, and the Making of Psychoanalysis*. New Haven: Yale University Press, 1989.
Gilman, Sander. *Freud, Race, and Gender*. Princeton, NJ: Princeton University Press, 1996.
Gondar, Josaida. *Os tempos de Freud*. Rio de Janeiro: Revinter, 1995.
Goux, Jean-Joseph. *El inconsciente freudiano y la revolución iconoclasta*. Buenos Aires: Letra Viva, 1993.
Graves, Robert, & Raphael Patai. *Hebrew Myths: The Book of Genesis*. New York: McGraw-Hill Book Company, 1966.
Grunfeld, Frederic V. *Prophets Without Honour: Freud, Kafka, Einstein, and Their World*. New York: McGraw-Hill, 1996.

Guinsburg, Jacó. *Aventuras de uma lingua errante: ensaios de literatura e teatro idiche*, São Paulo, Perspectiva, 1996.
Haddad, Gérard. *L'Enfant illégitime: sources talmudiques de la psychanalyse*. Paris: Hachette, 1981.
Harari, Roberto. *Lacan's Seminar on Anxiety: An Introduction*. New York: Other Press, 2001.
Hercenberg, Bernard. *L'Exil et la puissance d'Israël et du monde*. Arles: Actes Sud, 1990.
Jabès, Edmond. "Judaïsme et écriture." In Marie Moscivici & Jean-Michel Rey (eds.), *L'Écrit du temps*. Paris: Minuit, 1984.
Johnson, Paul. *A History of the Jews*. New York: HarperCollins Perennial Classics, 1988.
Jones, Ernest. *The Life and Works of Sigmund Freud*. Vol. 3: The Last Phase. New York: Basic Books, 1957.
Julien, Phillipe. *L'Étrange jouissance du prochain — science, ethique, religion*. Paris: Seuil, 1995.
Kant, Immanuel. *The Critique of Judgement*. In *World's Greatest Classic Books*. Corel Co., 1995.
Karl, Frederick. *Modern and Modernism: The Sovereignty of the Artist, 1885-1925*. New York: Harper, 1985.
Katz, Chaim Samuel. *Psicanálise e nazismo*. Rio de Janeiro: Taurus, 1985.
_____ *O coração distante: ensaio sobre a solidão positiva*. Rio de Janeiro: Revan, 1966.
_____ "Teoria e política na obra de Freud." *Tempo Brasileiro*, no. 70 *(Em torno de Freud)*. Rio de Janeiro, 1982.
Kaufmann, Pierre. *Dictionnaire de la psychanalyse*. Paris: Larousse, 1997.
Kohn, Max. *Freud et le yiddish: la préanalytique*. Paris: Christian Bourgois, 1982.
Koyré, Alexandre. *Études d'histoire de la pensée scientifique*, Paris: Gallimard, 1985.
Kristeva, Julia. *Tales of Love*. New York: Columbia University Press, 1989.
_____ *Strangers to Ourselves*. New York: Columbia University Press, 1994.
Krüll, Marianne. *Freud and His Father*. New York: W.W. Norton & Co., Inc. 1986.
Kuhn, Thomas. *The Structure of Scientific Revolutions*. Chicago: University of Chicago Press, 1970.
Lacan, Jacques. *Freud's Papers on Technique*. Ed. by Jacques-Alain Miller, trans. John Forrester. New York: W.W. Norton, 1988.
_____ *From an Other to the Other*. Privately translated by Cormac Gallagher.
_____ "Radiophonie." *Scilicet*. Paris: Seuil, 1968. Trans. Jack Stone. See http://web.missouri.edu/~stonej/Radiophonie.pdf
_____ "Proposition." *Scilicet*. Paris: Seuil, 1968. Trans. Russell Grigg, in *Analysis Number Six*. Melbourne: 1995.
_____ *The Other Side of Psychoanalysis*. Trans. Russell Grigg. New York: W.W. Norton. 2007
_____ *The Four Fundamental Concepts of Psychoanalysis*. Trans. Alan Sheridan. New York: W.W. Norton, 1998.
_____ *The Ethics of Psychoanalysis 1959-1960*. Trans. Dennis Porter. New York: W.W. Norton, 1992.
_____ *Television: A Challenge to the Psychoanalytic Establishment*. Trans. Jeffrey Mehlman. New York: W.W. Norton, 1993.
_____ *Écrits*. Trans. Bruce Fink, Heloise Fink, Russell Grigg. New York: W.W. Norton, 2006.
Lacoue-Labarthe, Phillipe, & Nancy, Jean-Luc, "Le people juive ne rêve pas," in Colloque de Montpellier, *La psychanalyse est-elle une histoire juive?* Paris: Seuil, 1980.
Lalande, André. *Vocabulaire technique et critique de la philosophie*. Paris: PUF, 1947.
Leclaire, Serge. *Le Pays de l'Autre*. Paris: Seuil, 1991.
Le Rider, Jacques. *Modernité viennoise et crises de l'identité*. Paris: PUF, 1990.
Lévinas, Emmanuel. *Totality and Infinity: An Essay on Exteriority*. Pittsburgh: Duquesne University Press, 1969.

Bibliography

_____ *Transcendence et inteligibilité*. Genève: Labor et Fides, 1984.
_____ *Humanisme de l'autre homme*. Paris : Fata Morgana,1972.
_____ *Quatre lectures talmudiques*. Paris: Éditions de Minuit, 1968.
_____ *Dieu, la mort et le temps*, Paris: Grasset, 1993.
_____ & Cohen, R. *Ethics and Infinity: Conversations with Philippe Nemo*. Pittsburgh: Duquesne University Press, 1985.
Lewis, Bernard. *The Middle East: A Brief History of the Last 2,000 Years*. New York: Scribner, 1995.
Löwy, Michel. *Redemption and Utopia: Libertarian Judaism in Central Europe*. Palo Alto: Stanford University Press, 1992.
Lyotard, Jean-François. "Figure forclose." In Marie Moscovici & Jean-Michel Rey (eds.), *L'Écrit du temps*. Paris: Minuit, 1984.
Malka, Salomon. *Lire Lévinas*. Paris: CERF, 1984.
Mannoni, Octave. *Freud*. New York: Pantheon Books, 1971.
Meghnagi, David (ed.). *Freud and Judaism*. London: Kamac Books, 1993.
Memmi, Albert. *L'Homme dominé*. Paris: Payot, 1973.
Mezan, Renato. *Psicanálise, judaísmo: ressonâncias*. São Paulo: Escuta, 1987.
Milner, Jean-Claude. *L'Oeuvre claire*. Paris: Seuil, 1995.
Monzani, Luiz Roberto. *Freud, o movimento de um pensamento*. Campinas: Unicamp, 1989.
_____ "L'étrangeté de l'étranger." In *Les grandes questions de la Philo*, Marie-Reine Morville (ed.). Paris: Maisonneuve et Larose, 1998.
Moscovici, Marie, & Rey, Jean-Michel (eds.). *L'Écrit du temps*. Paris: Minuit, 1984.
Nasio, Juan-David. *Five Lessons on the Psychoanalytic Theory of Jacques Lacan*, State Univ. of New York Press, 1998
Neher, André. "Vision du temps et de l'histoire dans la culture juive." In Paul Ricœur (ed.). *Cultures and Time*. Paris: The UNESCO Press, 1976.
Nicéas, Carlos Augusto. "Respostas ao saber suposto", in Jorge Forbes (org.), *Psicanálise ou psicoterapia*. Campinas: Papirus, 1997.
_____ "Uma questão de sobrevivência: notas sobre Freud e a IPA." In Jorge Forbes (org.), *A escola de Lacan: a formação do psicanalista e a transmissão da psicanálise*. Campinas: Papirus, 1984.
Ostow, Mortimer (ed.). *Judaism and Psychoanalysis*; New York: Ktav, 1982.
Ouaknin, Marc-Alain. *Le Livre brûlé: Lire le Talmude*. Paris: Lieu Commun, 1983. [*The Burnt Book: Reading the Talmud*. Princeton: Princeton University Press, 1995.]
Pfrimmer, Théo. *Freud lecteur de la Bible*. Paris: PUF, 1982.
Pommier, Gérard. *Naissance et renaissance de l'écriture*. Paris: PUF, 1993.
_____ "À propos de l'anti-semitisme." *Ornicar?* 24. Paris : Lyse, 1981.
Rabinovitch, Solal. "Écriture et défiguration, une lecture du *Moïse* de Freud." *Rue Descartes* 8/9. Paris: Albin Michel, 1993.
Regnault, François. *Dieu est inconscient*. Paris: Navarin, 1985.
Ricœur, Paul (ed.). *Cultures and Time. Les Cultures et le temps*. Paris: The UNESCO Press, 1976.
_____ & Jean Daniel. *Les grandes questions de la Philo*. Paris: Maisonneuve et Larose, 1998.
Robert, Marthe. *From Oedipus to Moses. Freud's Jewish Identity*. Littman Library of Jewish Civilization. 1997.
Roith, Estelle. *The Riddle of Freud: Jewish Influences on His Theory of Female Sexuality*. London: Routledge, 1987.
Rotker, Susana, Isaac Chocrón, & Elisa Lerner. *Los transgresores de la literatura venezolana*. Caracas: Fundarte, 1991.
Roudinesco, Elisabeth. *Jacques Lacan & Co.: A History of Psychoanalysis in France, 1925-1985*. Chicago: University of Chicago Press, 1990.

Rudge, Ana Maria. *Pulsão e linguagem: esboço de uma concepção psicanalítica do ato*. Rio de Janeiro: Jorge Zahar Editor, 1998.
Santiago, Silviano et al. *Glossário de Derrida*. Rio de Janeiro: Francisco Alves, 1976.
Santner, Eric L. *My Own Private Germany: Daniel Paul Schreber's Secret History of Modernity*. Princeton: Princeton University Press, 1996.
Schneider, Monique. "A proximidade de Lévinas e o *Nebenmensch* freudiano." *Caderno de Subjetividade* I/1, 1993, pp. 71-80.
Schorske, Carl E. *Fin-de-Siècle Vienna: Politics and Culture*. New York: Vintage, 1980.
Singer, Isaac Bashevis. *The Manor*. New York: Farrar; Straus and Giroux, 1967.
Souza, Paulo César de (ed.). *O gabinete do dr. Lacan*. São Paulo: Brasiliense, 1990.
Steiner, George. *In Bluebeard's Castle: Some Notes Towards the Redefinition of Culture*. New Haven: Yale University Press/London: Faber, 1971.
Taillander, Gerôme et al. *Les Identifications: Confrontation de la clinique et de la théorie de Freud à Lacan*. Paris: Editions de Noël, 1987.
Tort, Michel. "De l'interprétation ou la machine herméneutique." Paris: *Les Temps Modernes* 237, février-mars, 1966.
Trigano, Shmuel. *La Société juive à travers l'histoire*. Paris: Fayard, 1992.
Vernant, Jean-Pierre. *Myth and Thought among the Greeks*. Boston: Routledge and Kegan Paul, 1983.
Vieira, Nelson H. (ed.). *Construindo a imagem do judeu*. Rio de Janeiro: Imago, 1994.
Wiesel, Elie. *Night*. New York: Avon, 1969.
_____ *Paroles d'étranger*. Paris: Seuil, 1982.
_____ *All Rivers Run to the Sea: Memoirs*. New York: Schocken, 1996.
_____ "Por que escrevo?" In Vieira, Nelson H. (ed.). *Construindo a imagem do judeu*. Rio de Janeiro: Imago, 1994.
Wigoder, Geoffrey (ed). *Dictionnaire encyclopédique du judaïsme*. Paris: Editions du Cerf, 1993.
Winter, Jean-Pierre. "Transmission et Talmude." *Bulletin interne de l'EFP*, vol. II, June 1979.
Yerushalmi, Yosef Hayim. *Freud's Moses: Judaism Terminable & Interminable*. New Haven: Yale University Press, 1993.
_____ *Zakhor: Jewish History and Jewish Memory*. New York: Schocken, 1989.
Zaloszcyc, Armand. "Remarques sur la ségrégation constitutive du juif dans le nazisme." *La Lettre*, no. 2. Paris, 1993.
Zizek, Slavoj. *The Sublime Object of Ideology*. London/New York: Verso, 1989.

www.ingramcontent.com/pod-product-compliance
Lightning Source LLC
LaVergne TN
LVHW040154080526
838202LV00042B/3150